Happy Birthday, Chris.
Love from Dill. 2003
X X X

THE DAYS
OF MY FREEDOM

The Days of My Freedom

GRACE GRIFFITHS

with illustrations by

DAVID KNIGHT

WORLD'S WORK LTD

Published by World's Work Ltd
The Windmill Press, Kingswood, Tadworth, Surrey
Printed in Great Britain by
Cox & Wyman Ltd,
London, Fakenham and Reading
SBN 437 065006

For Doris

who made it possible

I

In which our dinner ran away, and a jackdaw died. Pots and pans. The witch who lived next door. Country remedies and traditional medicines. How my father earned a stubble goose.

"Dap'n on the 'aid, Missis. Dap'n on the 'aid," shouted the roadmender as the rabbit made off down our garden path. It was 1927, and meat was dear. My mother stood on the door-step wringing her hands as she watched our dinner stagger into the hedge across the road. The roadman switched off his tar spray and came over. What had happened? Where had the rabbit come from? Why had she not hit it on the head? he scolded. My mother explained that a friend had brought it from the harvest field, and had left it on the kitchen table thinking he had killed it with a blow from his ash stick. But the animal was merely stunned. As soon as it had recovered consciousness, it ran away. She was almost in tears.

The roadmender begged her not to worry and trotted back to the small tent which housed his tools. Presently he emerged with a shotgun. He aimed at the top of the elm trees opposite our cottage; two rooks fell at his shot. The third bird to flutter down was a jackdaw. When he brought it to us with the other birds, I burst into tears. It was my pet Jack, who slept in the linhay with the cats. I had found him a year before lying injured by the roadside, and had nursed him back to health. One wing was slightly deformed and one eye socket was empty. The remaining bright blue eye was already glazed over, but it was unmistakably my Jack.

My mother alternately berated the man for killing my pet and thanked him for providing meat for the pot. For one horrified moment I feared that she intended to cook Jack.

The noise of the shots and loud voices brought George Harris from the cottage next door, and my father from his bed. Dad had been gassed in the war and was a permanent invalid. His lungs were rotted by chlorine, and he often had great difficulty in breathing. Even so, he rounded on the roadman, who stood holding his reeking gun, telling him that he had no right to be shooting so near the two cottages. My mother broke in with the full story, and George Harris opined that it was impossible to tell a jackdaw from a rook in the "tops o' thiccy trees". Accusations and explanations went on for a long time but eventually all was settled amicably. The roadmender went slowly back to his tar spraying. As he walked off I was fascinated to notice that he was pigeon-toed.

My father and mother went into our stone-flagged kitchen, and my mother put the kettle on the open fire in the middle of the kitchen range. She placed a brown china tea-pot to warm on the hob. My father started skinning the rooks. Jack was left on the front door-step.

Unable to bear any more, I ran down the path, past George Harris's stack of wood-faggots, into the field behind the house. When I reached the grass I slowed up, and walked with my toes turned in like the roadman.

The grass was long and dry, and the seeds from it fell inside my sandals. An occasional thistle scratched my knees.

The field sloped to a brook which came brown and peaty down from Dartmoor. It flowed between deep banks topped with bracken, gorse and brambles. In one place the banks levelled out and the stream spilled into a wide, shallow pool. This was where the cows came to drink, and the ground on either side was poached by their hooves. Large flat stones had been laid at intervals across the pool so that it was possible to cross dry shod, but I ignored the stones, and hoisting my cotton dress about my waist, I took off my sandals and picked my way across the mud and cow-pats into the water. My footwear buckled together by their straps and slung about my neck, I set off ankle deep down stream. Soon I was hidden between high banks. Small brown trout and silvery minnows darted away ahead of me. The sun was hot on my head and the water cool over my feet. I saw a horse-leech lurking in the shallows and gave it a wide berth. I knew all about horse-leeches, having met them before in this very stream.

Where the brook passed through the hedge that bounded the field I climbed out of the water. A wild cherry tree, its branches hung with bright red fruit, grew out of the hedge. I knew that the cherries were not fit to eat; the flesh was thin and bitter, covering a hard stone, but I did not find this particularly disappointing since I had never tasted the cultivated variety.

The tree was my hide-out. In spring, I sat among the pale pink blossoms; in summer, I climbed the sticky branches to hide behind the curtain of leaves; in autumn, the leaves were sparse and yellowing but the clusters of fruit gave cover enough. In winter, the tree was bare and cold, too exposed to the winds which swept down from the moor for me to want to climb it.

Beyond the hedge the valley sloped down through a patchwork of gold and green fields to a blue line which I believed to be the sea. Behind me Dartmoor stretched as a long line of hills. The rounded hump of Cawsand Beacon, still streaked with red where the heather had not completely faded, dominated the skyline. Here and there patches of pale smoke drifted across the hills where the farmers had lit swaling fires to clear their land of dead heather and bracken in order to ensure a lusty springtime growth.

From the moor a road wound down to our cottages and far out on it I could see the movement of a vehicle. It was, it must be, the tinkers.

These itinerant craftsmen came regularly every autumn in a horse-drawn wagon, visiting every house and cottage between Okehampton and Exeter. They mended leaking kettles and saucepans, "soddering" them as they said with white-hot tin, bought rabbit skins and mole skins which the thrifty country folk had pegged out to dry on the walls and fences, sold new pots, crockery, knives, forks and spoons, and carried news from village to village. Their visit was an exciting event, and I lost no time in running home to warn my parents of their arrival.

The tinkers did not reach us until late afternoon. My father, exhausted by all the excitement, had gone back to bed. My mother had a frying-pan to be mended, and wanted to buy a new kettle.

While the haggling was going on I fed the horse with small potatoes. This was not a very satisfactory ploy for either the horse or myself, since as soon as the animal lowered its head and parted its soft rubbery lips to suck the food from the palm of my hand, the sight of those long, yellow teeth proved too much for my courage and I dropped the potatoes on the ground. Tethered by a short rope to our garden fence the horse had some difficulty in reaching the food, and only managed to lip up one or two of the delicacies. Soon, both the horse and I were thoroughly fed up with each other, so I climbed into the wagon to inspect the contents.

Rows and rows of shining pans hung from the sides of the vehicle under the arched canvas roof. The tinker's boy had been left in charge while his father heated his soldering irons in a small fire, kindled with the aid of a paraffin-soaked rag in an iron pan by the roadside. Deftly he handled the soldering iron, the flux hissed, and soon there was a bright new patch on the side of our blackened frying-pan. My mother called to me to choose the new kettle from the selection the tinker's boy showed me. I choose one which had a cap on its spout; the boy said it whistled when it boiled. My mother quibbled at this; the whistling kettle cost one shilling and six-pence—the others only cost one shilling and three pence. After some argument we bought the dearer kettle for cash and paid for the repair to the frying-pan with a handful of smelly rabbit skins.

The tinker told my mother some spicy items of local news and, in her turn, she enquired after some friends in North Tawton and Okehampton.

The Harrises were not buying from the tinkers, but four-year-old Jimmy Harris sat on the steps of the van, watching. By the time our business was concluded twilight was falling, and Jimmy and I clung to our front fence to see the wagon go out of sight down the long, straight road that led to Bow, and then to Copplestone, Crediton and Exeter.

I was two years older than Jimmy, but he and his brother Derek were the only children with whom I had any regular contact. Today, Derek would be labelled spastic but in those days his disease had no name. He sat all day long strapped into a wooden chair. His hands drooped from the wrist so that he was unable to pick up or hold anything, his feet chattered constantly on the ground, and he made uncouth sounds with his mouth, dribbling saliva continually down the front of his jersey. He was incontinent and smelly, but I often played with him for lack of other companionship.

Jimmy Harris was a plump rosy-cheeked urchin who followed me everywhere. He was remarkably gullible and would allow me to seat him on an ant-hill because I said it was a fairy throne, or would fill his pockets with sheeps' droppings which I persuaded him were marbles.

Old Mrs. Worden, their grandmother, lived in the cottage with her daughter Emma, her son-in-law George, and Derek and Jimmy. She was old and bent and very dirty. Local folk believed her to be a witch, and the power of her evil eye was a thing to be feared. When offended she foamed at the mouth and slobbered curses on people or "ootched" them as she called it. She "ootched" our cats because she said they raided her chicken-run, but my father, a Londoner who did not subscribe to the country superstitions, told her that bad wishes would come home to roost. Sure enough, several of Mrs. Worden's fowls died of the gapes and thereafter she behaved towards my father with the respect due to one whose magic was greater than her own.

My mother, who was Devon born and bred, was uncertain how to treat Mrs. Worden, and alternately placated and derided her. The old woman was very fond of children, and was exceptionally kind to me. I had been a delicate baby, and my upbringing to the age of six years had been assisted by the potions and medicaments that Mrs. Worden concocted. She came and rubbed my chest with a compound of goose-grease and wild mint when I had bronchitis. She pounded the fleshy leaves of pennywort into a green paste to soothe my sore eyes. She bound pieces of mouldy cheese over my torn shins, and covered my back with brown paper, and then ironed it with a hot iron, when I had a chesty cold. When I had whooping cough she had begged my mother to take me out into the fields, to rouse a sheep from its sleep, and to lay me down on the grass still warm from the animal's body. My mother refused to do this, and the doctor was called instead. This was an event, for doctor's bills were expensive and were to be avoided whenever possible. I had caught scarlet fever during the previous summer and this would have been a financial disaster if Dr. Rowse-Bastard had ever sent us his bill. As it was, the expense was considerable although I had been allowed to stay at home sealed into the bedroom with my mother who had nursed me. Necessary food and medicines were passed to us through the open window by my father who stood on the downstairs window-sill. Reports on my condition were made to the doctor verbally, again through the window, by my mother. She also handed out to my father the covered slop-pails which we used for our toilet.

After six weeks, when I had finished peeling, the door was unsealed and we were let out. The whole cottage was fumigated. My convalescence had been hastened by gifts of the brownest eggs from Mrs. Worden's hens, and dishes of raspberries laced with thick cream which she herself scalded over her kitchen fire from the raw cream that was part of George Harris's perks as a hedger on Mr. Joslin's farm. Their cottage was "tied" and so rent free. George earned thirty shillings per week: his perks included free milk, an annual ham and a share of any surplus "beastings", the thick colostrum milk a cow gives immediately after the birth of a calf. The beastings were greatly prized since it was only necessary to sprinkle a dish of the milk with sugar, and cook it slowly in the oven, to produce a custard as rich and solid as cheese-cake.

Mrs. Worden was illiterate and the Harrises could read and write only with great difficulty. They all stood in awe of my father and mother who were "eddicated", read books and newspapers and could write letters.

My father acted as scribe to many of the local folk. They came from far and near with their problems—a son in Australia who should be told some family news, an aunt who must be informed of a death in the family. A local farrier, whose income was so high that he had to pay four or five pounds per year in income tax, came every April to have his tax forms filled in. He, like the others, paid in kind, and our standard of living was improved by gifts of home-cured bacon, black puddings made from the fresh blood of a pig, chitterlings, brawn and the occasional boiling-hen.

Someone once gave us a stubble goose. This was an out of season treat since normally we only had goose at Christmas—a gift from my grandfather. The autumn goose, fattened on the grain left among the stubble in the field after the wheat had been harvested, was fatter and more tender than the geese reared for Christmas. My mother pricked the flesh all over to let out the excess fat, and cooked the bird by hanging it from a hook in the roof of the oven; it was too big to fit in any other way. We had sprouts and carrots, boiled potatoes and a dish of baked apples with it and were too full to eat the baked egg custard and bottled plums which were to have been our second course.

2

Why I walked pigeon-toed, and sought an omen in the sky. Books, reading and Sunday hymns. Goat's milk. The Old Men of the moor. From workhouse to workhouse—Sammy Gough and a runaway horse. The village smithy and bakery.

The roadmender was working on the stretch of road outside our cottage for several days after the death of my pet jackdaw, and I grew very friendly with him. Privately, I nicknamed him "Pigeon Toes", and mimicked his walk so often that it became habitual to me. My parents were very worried about this, and did not connect my new gait with "Pigeon Toes". I was marched into Bow village to my grandmother who was puzzled but decided that "It'll pass, Edie, the cheel'll get over it". The visit to the village was so exciting that on the way home I forgot and walked normally. My mother suddenly put two and two together; I was soundly slapped, and sent to bed early in disgrace. It was autumn, and the evenings were growing dark. Dimly from my window I could see over the field to the brook and farther to where the land ran up to the moor. The distance was blue and hazy, and the tors were dark jagged shapes against the pale sky. My father had recently told me the story of Romulus and Remus and the building of Rome, and how the two brothers had sought an augury in the sky. I was bored and miserable so I told myself that if I were to squeeze my eyes tight shut, spit and cross my toes, then open my eyes suddenly I, too, might see an omen in the sky. If I did, it would mean that tomorrow would be a happy day.

I squeezed my eyes shut, moistened my finger with spittle, and made the sign of a cross on my toes, then flipped up my eyelids to peer at the night sky. There silhouetted against the wine-dark moors, was a gleaming silver bird. It flew slowly across the sky, and dropped suddenly behind a patch of trees. I had my omen—a seagull caught in the last, long rays of the setting sun was to me something strange and wonderful. I went to bed comforted, assured of a happy day on the morrow. Not long afterwards my father crept into the room with a book in his hand, and I knew I was forgiven when he read to me from our tattered copy of Hans Andersen's fairy tales.

My mother ran the local County Library centre. Three boxes of library books were sent to Bow school at regular intervals. My mother was responsible for lending them to those who wished to read. Naturally, we had first choice of the reading matter. My father read westerns and detective novels, popular science and theology. My mother read standard fiction and biographies. I read whatever I could get hold of—school stories, adventures and even the occasional adult novel. I had been able to read since the age of four, and even three syllable words presented no difficulty to me. I did not understand everything that I read but could always master the gist of a story and that was all that mattered.

In winter, when, as the village folk would say, "the waters were out"—meaning the stream between us and the village had broken its banks and made the roadway impassable, we sat as a family around the kitchen table and read evening after evening by the light of the Aladdin oil-lamp. If my father was poorly we lit the Valor oil-heater in the big bedroom and read beside his bed. Sometimes, bored by my book, I stared at the Aladdin lamp until my eyes grew tired of the brilliance of the incandescent mantle and my lids dropped. Glowing mantles in a succession of brilliant colours floated across a backdrop of darkness, each one a little less bright than the one before, until they faded out, pale ghosts of the original. If my parents realized what I was doing I was severely scolded for ruining my eyes. "You'll be sorry one day, you will. Just you wait and see."

Reading was not our only entertainment. On Sunday evenings

my mother played hymns on our upright piano and sometimes my father sang. To save oil we lit the candles in the brass holders protruding from the pleated yellow satin which covered the front of the piano above the keyboard. I was not allowed to sing because I had never mastered "pitch" and wandered happily from key to key. After a while, bored by the weekly repetitions of "The Old Rustic Cross", "Beulah Land" or "Crown Him Lord of All", I would wait for a pause in the music and sneak up to the piano to play my own little tuneless tune on the highest notes of the treble clef. Immediately I was soundly slapped and banished upstairs.

Although I was six years old I had not yet gone to school for more than a few odd days. The walk to Bow village was a long one and I was delicate. My grandmother said that I was anaemic and suggested a diet of goat's milk, raw liver and chopped raw vegetables. A goat was somehow procured from a local farmer and tethered by a long chain to a stake at the end of our garden. My mother struggled to milk it but it was a very evil creature, and as often as not kicked over the can of milk as soon as she had finished. I tried to fondle it but it took an instant dislike to me and usually butted me flat. Once I managed to dodge past it to stand by the stake to which it was fastened. Immediately the wily animal walked round and round me until it had me bound firmly to the post with its chain, and we were held in enforced proximity. Furthermore it butted me with its head and tried to bite my fingers. I could not move, and it was almost two hours before my father looked for me in the garden, finding me in tears, still tied to the stake. After that Nanny went, and I had to do without my goat's milk, but the raw liver and vegetables did me good.

It was suggested that I might go to school regularly in the following year. Meanwhile my father gave me lessons. He taught me to write and to do simple sums. When he was well enough we cadged lifts in passing pony traps and walked on the moor around Okehampton. He helped me to find tiny flint arrow heads—"elf bolts"—in the ruined Bronze Age hut circles. He told me stories about the medieval tin-miners, about plagues and fires, plants and trees. In this way I learned quite a lot of history, some geography and a smattering of geology and botany. My knowledge was patchy and often incorrect, but very exciting. For me, the Old Men of the moor lived, they were real people whose hardships and pleasures I felt that I understood. They were my friends.

I tried to pass on my learning to Derek Harris, and spent hours trying to get him to repeat the alphabet after me, but he could only make gurgling noises while the spittle ran down his chin. Looking back, I think he could understand a fair amount of what I said to him, and did his best to reply, but was unable to control his vocal chords and his tongue enough to frame the words. He certainly enjoyed our lessons: when I went away he beat on his knees with his nerveless hands and stamped his feet angrily on the ground.

My interest in history was given more impetus by a gentleman called John Green. Mr. Green was a tramp who regularly passed our way on his journey from Exeter workhouse to Okehampton workhouse and back again. Our cottage was on the main road between these two lodging-houses at which down-and-outs were allowed to stay for one night only. Some of them walked from Exeter to Okehampton, Okehampton to Exeter, ceaselessly the year round. There were many vagrants on the roads in those days, a large number of them were men of good education who were unable to obtain work. Some had fought in the First World War, and were unable or unwilling to settle into the scheme of things on their return to civilian life. The distance from Exeter to Okehampton was about twenty-five miles. The journey could be broken at Crediton, but this was only nine miles from Exeter, and left a long trek without lodging for the next day. In summer, many of them slept rough. In winter, footsore and weary, they passed our cottage as they pressed on towards Okehampton. Often they stopped to beg food or a night's lodging in our linhay. My parents never refused them bread and cheese or sometimes a hard-boiled egg, and a billet of straw to sleep on in the outhouse. The tramps made their own tea, brewing up in a billycan over a tiny fire which they lit on the earth floor. Sometimes they carried a grubby half-empty tin of condensed milk; sometimes my mother gave them fresh milk.

I was forbidden to have anything to do with our down-at-heel guests, but I usually managed to pass a few words with them. Mr. Green I knew well because my parents liked him and brought him into the kitchen. He had been a teacher before he became a tramp, and he told me many stories of school life. He was also keenly interested in the derivation of words and place names. It was he who told me that Silver Street—the name given to the cottages in which we and the Harrises lived—was not, as I supposed, the name of the last surviving street of a long-lost village. He explained that the word "street" came from the Latin word "strata" or paved way and that no doubt the long, straight road running past our front door was an ancient highway by which the silver-coloured tin was brought down from the moor, and taken to Exeter. He peopled the road with ghosts.

I loved Mr. Green, and when one autumn he came no more I felt I had really lost a friend.

Another vagrant friend of mine was Sammy Gough. Sammy was not strictly a tramp; he had a caravan somewhere on the other side of North Tawton, but he tramped the roads picking up odds and ends to sell. We always thought he was very poor. Often he persuaded me to nip over a hedge to pull a swede for him or to fetch a few carrots from our garden. Whenever I did this he gave me a penny—far more than the goods were worth. He begged scraps of soap from my mother and she always saved for him the soggy pieces from the bottom of the soap-dish. I used to walk a hundred yards or so with him down the road, and he once told me that he melted the soap down to make tablets to sell. Years later, when I was in my teens, I heard that Sammy had died leaving a small fortune in pound notes hidden in his caravan.

Sammy always seemed to me to be very old but I suppose he was only in his middle forties at the time I knew him. He was certainly very active, and taught me how to play leapfrog. He frequently ate his lunch—a hunk of bread and a wedge of cheese—high up in the elm trees opposite our cottage. He said he liked the view. I could never climb as high as he so I stood underneath, and we held a shouted conversation. He taught me weather lore:

When Cosdon (Cawsand) is swathed in grey mist, there's rain sweeping down from the moor;
When the sun shines through a break in the clouds, making a slide of light, there will be showers for twenty-four hours;
When the river runs brown and clear, fine weather is coming;
When the gnats fly low, a heatwave is on the way.

Once he showed me where a rainbow bent into the ground in the corner of a field of barley, and I went and stood in the multi-coloured light with stripes of red, orange and blue running down my body. I expected to come out a changed person, but I still looked the same when the rainbow faded. My cotton dress with the huge brown butterfly embroidered across the chest looked just as drab as ever.

One day Sammy Gough was perched high in the elm trees and I was scuffling about in the dry leaves at the foot when we heard the sound of galloping hooves. Horses were commonplace on our road—cars were still a rarity—but few people galloped except on the moors. Sammy swung out on to a branch, and peered up the North Tawton road. Suddenly he dropped to the ground. The hoof-beats were now a lot nearer, and there was a strange, swishing sound with them. Telling me to stay where I was, Sammy moved into the road just as a fine blue-roan cob came into view. He was galloping madly, his head flung back, his eyes wild. A large hazel branch tied to his reins dragged along the road between his forefeet. Obviously he had been tethered to a hedge and had torn himself free. Frightened, he had set off; the branch dragging between his hooves had completed his panic. It would be only a matter of time before the branch tangled with his legs and he was brought down with a broken limb.

As he went by Sammy leaped for the reins and hung on. The cob reared and snorted but slowed its mad rush, and finally drew to a halt. Sammy gentled him and freed the branch. In no time at all the animal was snatching nettles from the hedge. I patted his muzzle but Sammy told me to leave him alone since he might still be nervous. Sammy thought that he belonged to a farmer a few miles up the road, and after a while he rode off in that direction.

Runaway horses were by no means uncommon. Often in the evenings when I had gone to bed I would hear the drum of hooves going past the cottage. The horse would have been left outside a pub tethered to a branch or to railings and would have broken loose. The commonest accidents on the roads were those which involved horses—not motor vehicles. Usually someone was thrown from his horse, and since the average countryman did not wear protective head-gear, he suffered a fractured skull or, at least, severe concussion. Sometimes a horse-drawn trap would overturn, killing or maiming its occupants.

A motor-car in Devon in the 1920's was something to be wondered at. The doctor in Bow village had a Bean which he used to park carefully outside our front gate on the few occasions that he visited our cottage. I could never understand why the machine, which roared up the road with such speed and power, stood silent and still while the doctor was in our house and, if I was not the patient, I watched anxiously from the safety of my bedroom window in case the car burst into life of its own accord and made off down the road.

Once when I was recovering from a very bad attack of measles, Doctor Rowse-Bastard took me with him for a little spin across the moors. The ride was a cross between agony and ecstasy—my fear of the vehicle was only just held in check by my delight in the swift, effortless movement.

Very occasionally, a bi-plane would rumble across the sky above the cottages. The sound brought both families running to their doors to stare at the wonderful machine. My father told us tales of the zeppelin raids on London during the war, and how four houses in a street had been destroyed by one bomb. He told us, too, of seeing a zeppelin brought down in flames. Then he spoke of his time in the trenches, the mud, the poor food and the bitter cold. Later he sang me to sleep with soldiers' songs—"It's a Long Way to Tipperary", "Keep the Home Fires Burning" and "Goodbye Dolly Gray", which I afterwards learned was a relic of the Boer War. The poppies growing thick in the ripening corn always reminded him of "over there" and, walking through the fields, he told me many stories of heroism and comradeship which fired my imagination for years to come. He had been gassed in 1916 in the Battle of the Somme, and the doctors had told him that he had only two years to live. In 1918 he had met and married my mother. They had moved to Devon for what they thought would be his final months. In 1921 I was born and my father, holding me in his arms, had vowed that he would live until I was thirty. He did just that.

From my earliest years I knew my father was ill, and that he might not live long, and that it was all the fault of those wicked Germans. In very wet winters, water in the field behind our cottage drained into our kitchen covering the floor an inch deep. I once heard my mother saying that it must bring germs with it. This worried me a lot because I equated germs with Germans. I often crept downstairs when my parents had gone to bed to look under the dresser to make sure no Germans were lurking there.

The transition from London to the depths of the country must have been hard for my father, but for me, Silver Street was heaven. I loved the fields and the outdoor life I led. I loved also to visit Bow village and especially to go to the smithy and the bakery.

To pass through the wide doors of the forge was like entering the gates of hell. Smoke made the interior murky and the figures of the smith and his boy, devils with tridents, were outlined against the glow of the fire as they heated a strip of iron, held in long pincers, till the metal shone white hot. Moving in unison they flung the iron on the anvil and hammered it out. Then it was heated again until it was malleable enough to bend around a wooden wheel. As soon as the wheel was shod, the whole was flung into a trough of cold water where it hissed and threw up clouds of pungent-smelling steam. A few more touches with hammer and a metal file, and the wheel, with its bright, new rim was ready to be knocked into place on the trap to which it belonged.

There were usually one or two horses waiting to be shod in the yard behind the smithy, and the boy brought them in, one at a time, when the smith was ready for them. Frequent visits to the smithy had taught the animals that they had nothing to fear, and they stood patiently on three legs while the smith unclinched the nails which held the old shoe. I held my breath while the hoof was filed down and winced when the new shoe, hot from the fire, was nailed into place. But it was all quickly done. Soon the horse was clattering away over the cobbles, the hair of its fetlocks a little singed, but otherwise none the worse for its adventure.

Next to the smithy, the baker's shop was to me the most exciting place in the village.

The baker, Mr. Hodge, helped by young Gordon Yelland, kneaded yeasty-smelling dough on a long, floured table. Sometimes they stretched the bread into long strips, sometimes they pummelled it with their fists or pounded it with their elbows. Behind them a huge, black oven stood above a furnace which Gordon fed from time to time with lumps of coal and faggots of wood. When the bread was ready the oven doors were opened and the previous batch of hot loaves were removed on a long-handled shovel. The newly shaped loaves were put into the oven and the doors were clanged shut.

Gordon Yelland, who was only a few years older than I, went with Mr. Hodge to deliver the bread to the outlying farms and cottages. Their wagon, drawn by a fat skewbald pony, had a hooped canvas roof under which the bread was stacked on wooden shelves. They also carried with them trays of currant buns, lardy cakes and small, fancy iced cakes. Gordon's day started at five and often did not end until ten o'clock in the evening.

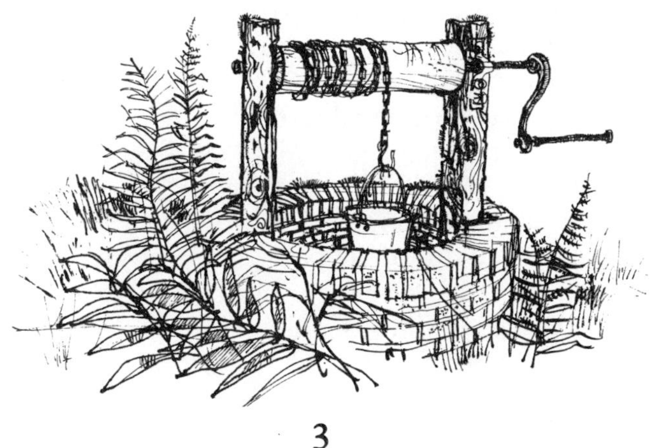

3

When my father drank farm-house cider. The cottages then and now. Sweet well water. Why Jimmy Harris ate tommy-totties. Lessons learned at school. I made a plasticine dog and suffered the consequences. First love.

We paid two shillings and sixpence a week for our cottage. I knew because sometimes I was sent to Mr. Joslin's farm at Burston to pay the rent. The farm was two miles distant by road but only about half a mile if you crossed the brook at the bottom of the field, ran across another field, and went through the orchards behind the farm-house. Farmer Joslin had a cider-press in his farm-yard, and every autumn the cider apples were gathered from the orchards together with any windfalls which lay beneath the trees, and fed into the press. The apples were indescribably filthy, and were well mixed with dead leaves, grass and hen droppings but as Mrs. Joslin said, "It's all cleaned in the ferment." Children were not encouraged to watch cider-making, probably because when the great wooden press began to tighten, accidents could easily happen.

The cider made on Devon farms in those days was used mainly for home consumption. The hands in the harvest fields were plentifully supplied from a keg kept in the shade of the hedge. The farmer too had kegs put by for his own use. If possible he stored his drink in rum-casks and after a few months it became extremely potent.

When my father first came to Devon he was regarded by the local as a "townie" and something of a joke since he knew little of country ways. When he was well enough he enjoyed a glass of beer at the Burston Inn but would never touch cider as he thought it a drink for boys. One evening he went with some friends to play cards at the Joslins' farm, and there, because good manners demanded it, he drank the farmer's cider.

I remember well my mother's fury when my father was helped home by two friends just after midnight. He was singing loudly, and the noise brought me to the head of the stairs. Dad was man-handled into bed by his friends, and my mother rolled herself up in a rug, and slept in a chair. After that he treated cider with some respect.

Farmer Joslin was a good friend to us. Our cottage would normally have been let to one of his farm-hands—George Harris next door was his hedger and ditcher—but it was the 1920's, and Mr. Joslin was employing a minimum labour force. He had known my mother since his boyhood, and when he heard that she and her family needed a home—we were living at that time in temporary accommodation in Bow village—he had offered us the cottage. It was very small. The front door opened directly into a square kitchen, stone-flagged, with one recessed window overlooking the front garden and main road. The stairs, with their steep wedge-shaped treads, led from the kitchen to a small landing between two bedrooms. The landing window overlooked the field behind, the bedroom windows looked out on to the front garden. The kitchen range was the only heating, the lighting was from oil-lamps, and water had to be fetched from a well sunk between the two cottages. An earth closet was in the linhay alongside the house.

I was forbidden to go near the well which was reputed to be eighty feet deep and was only covered by a rotting wooden lid. There was no wall nor safety railing, and the windlass with its rusty chain and iron handle was the only thing to cling to when lowering the galvanized bucket to the water. If you were not very careful the weight of the bucket pulled the chain too rapidly off the roller, and the handle of the windlass would fly round and deal you a fearsome blow on the head. The water, however, was excellent. It came from a spring deep down in the rock on which the cottages were built and no matter how long the summer drought the bucket always came up filled to the brim with cool sparkling water that tasted clean and fresh.

One winter, when work was slack on the farm, our landlord had the well cleaned out. I watched from the bedroom window. Bucket after bucket of thick black mud came up and was tipped into a manure cart. As the water drained from the mud the bleached bones of small animals could be seen buried in it. I listened in fascinated horror as the men hazarded their guesses. "That was a cat, I reckon," one said. Another picked out a pointed skull. "That's a rat's 'aid."

As well as mud and bones the bucket brought up a shrunken and felted trilby hat and big, black, slimy slugs which must have been clinging to the sides of the shaft near the water-line. I had never seen such slugs.

Eventually the well was pronounced clean. A brand new bucket was attached to the rusty chain, the cogs that controlled the handle were oiled, and the well went into use again. The water tasted just the same—no better, no worse, but for several weeks my mother insisted on boiling it, although my father said this was shutting the stable door when the horse had bolted. After a while we forgot all about the cleaning of the well, and drank the water as freely as before.

Many years later I went back to Silver Street. The two cottages, together with part of the outbuildings, had been made into one large house. The old straw thatch had been replaced by slates. The doors, which formerly opened as two halves, a top half and a bottom half, were now in one piece and modern in design. The well was closed in and a pump stood where the windlass had been. The road in front of the cottages had been widened so that the front garden was curtailed, and in what used to be the Harris's garden there stood a modern greenhouse.

In the old days Farmer Joslin was always ready to improve his property. When the two cottages had been flooded more often than usual one winter by drainage from the field, he set George Harris to work digging a deep ditch along the back of the buildings to take the surplus water. This worked admirably and our kitchens were reasonably dry thereafter. The ditch itself, to my delight, became the haunt of frogs, and in spring there were masses of pale spawn deposited in it. I told Jimmy Harris that this was wild tapioca pudding, and he ate quite a lot of it before he was sick. When his mother found out what had happened, she collared me and gave me a sound beating, "Vor a' makin' of Jimmy tu ate tommy-totties," (tadpoles).

This led to a state of war between my family and the Harrises because my parents maintained that whatever I had done, punishment should only be meted out by them. Mrs. Worden was at that time at loggerheads with her daughter and son-in-law otherwise we should have been "ootched". For a whole summer I was forbidden to play with Derek and Jimmy and in the autumn I was sent to school regularly. I was eight and a half years old.

Bow Council School had been erected towards the end of the last century. The drabness of its brick walls was only relieved by the sickly pea-green of the doors and window-frames. Pointed iron railings of the same green enclosed an asphalt playground, a bicycle shed and lavatories for boys and girls. The head-master, Mr. A. J. Pyne, who had very up-to-date teaching methods, was fairly new to his job. He was assisted by his wife and two other teachers—one of whom, Ethel Folley, was a cousin of my mother by marriage.

I was put in Standard One. We sat two to a desk in a small class-room jutting off the main body of the school. On the window-sills were pots of wild flowers which the children had brought: on the walls were maps and, horror of horrors, an artist's impression of how the world came into being—first a red-hot mass of molten rock, then the formation of the seas and continents, the appearance of primeval life, dinosaurs and the first men, and a diagram, covering millions of years, showing Darwin's theory of evolution. This was heady stuff. I hardly dared look at it because I knew the world and all things in it had come into being in seven days—it said so in the Bible. To think anything else was blasphemy.

I kept shooting scared glances at the walls throughout my first week, and spent more time thinking about the things portrayed than I did about the daily lessons which, in truth, I found easy enough. I could read and write and do sums better than any of the other children in the class, and my knowledge of geography and history, although patchy, was wide. By the end of the first week I had come to a sort of compromise whereby on one plane I accepted the Bible story implicitly and on the other I believed in the theory of evolution and all that it entailed. I made no attempt to reconcile the two beliefs. On the whole I liked the Darwinian theory the better—it was so much more exciting—but I felt guilty about this.

I was on good terms with Ethel Folley but came to grief with Mrs. Pyne because I hated sewing and my knitting was a disgrace. We had to make pillow-slips in the sewing class; the calico was stiff and difficult to get a needle through; my seams were grubby, and the stitches looked like cats' teeth. I started to knit a kettle holder in bright red knitting-cotton; I began with thirty stitches and ended with twenty-three and quite a number of holes. I liked raffia work and happily wove a table mat for my mother, and I was quite clever with plasticine but this was my downfall. One afternoon we were allowed to model anything we liked and, as I owned a dog, I settled down to shape a faithful likeness of him. Unfortunately, I did not realize that some details were better omitted. The boy next to me—Alan Rushton—son of the Congregational minister, noticed, and announced the fact in a loud voice. Mrs. Pyne writing at her desk heard the giggles that were spreading through the class, and came to investigate. Her furious reaction to my handiwork was a mystery to me, and when she crumpled the model in her hands and ordered me to go and stand in the corner, I felt unjustly treated.

Mrs. Pyne kept me in after school, and made me write on the blackboard in my best handwriting "I must not be rude" as many times as I could until I had filled both sides of the board.

I did not understand what the fuss was all about, and when I reached home I could not really tell my parents why I had been kept in. My mother went to the school next day, and explanations were made. Both my parents seemed to think that I had been unfairly dealt with, but the incident was soon forgotten.

Being kept in after school was, for me, a disaster. It meant that I had to walk home alone since the other children who lived in the direction of my home had already left. I had an absurd fear of steam-rollers, and if I heard one in the distance would climb a hedge and run over the fields rather than meet it. I was also afraid of Butcher Sanders who had a shop at the lower end of the village. His daughter Brenda sat next to me in Standard One and, if I offended her, would say that she would tell her Dad, and he would slit my throat with his butcher's knife. I thought he was quite capable of this—I had heard the pigs squealing in his yard on slaughter-day. Once he had come to Silver Street to kill some hens he had bought from Mrs. Worden. He had seized each bird in his ham-like hands, and thrust a small knife into its gaping beak, cutting through the roof of the mouth into the brain. The corpse, flung aside on a pile of its fellows, had twitched and kicked for several minutes. I therefore ran very fast past Butcher Sanders' shop, and did not stop until I was safely across the stone arch of Bow Bridge.

School taught me that everyone was not equal. I was quick to notice that some of us were brighter, cleaner, better-fed and better-dressed than the others and that we had more of the teacher's attention. It was not favouritism; in the time available Mrs. Pyne did the best she could for all of us, but a few children were almost unteachable. Children from some of the outlying hamlets came clad in ill-fitting cast-offs, wore shoes or boots with leaky soles, and had permanent, snuffly colds. They were usually members of large families whose father, a farm-labourer, did not earn enough to support his brood, and whose mother, dragged down by perpetual pregnancies, was too busy trying to find food in an empty cupboard to keep her children clean and tidy. The children often had lice in their hair and patches of impetigo on their cheeks. Two little girls from such a family who sat at the back of my class were sewn into their underwear for warmth each winter. A kind of flannel binder was wound round and round each child's body and their vests or combinations were stitched to this so that there was no possibility of a draught reaching their skin. On top they wore a variety of ragged petticoats, and a dress or skirt and torn jumper. The outside clothes were washed occasionally but the smell from their underwear, by the time spring came, was indescribable. My mother told me that when she was a little girl, to be sewn into your clothes for the winter was the rule rather than the exception.

I fell in love that year for the first time. The object of my affections was a boy called Percy Madge who was older than I. Percy sometimes brought a pet ferret to school in his jacket pocket. It was a beautiful little animal, pale gold in colour, with a pink snout, pink eyes and pink tipped ears. A tiny plaited silk muzzle covered its jaws. Percy would let me stroke the creature and even hold it on my lap while he clutched the end of the silken leash. The warm sinuous body pulsed with life. The bright little eyes peered up at me enquiringly—I loved the ferret. I thought I loved Percy too. But he was a big boy and found my adoration embarrassing. He called me "Skinny Legs".

4

Friends at Hampson Farm. Broadnymet Moor and the ruined church. The Broadnymet ghost. Pixie lanterns and gypsy friends. My fortune was told.

Each morning, before I went to school, it was my job to fetch the milk from Hampson farm. The milk can was a conical tin pot about ten inches deep with a close-fitting lid and a loop of wire for a handle, which I swung from my hand. Ours was a plain tin receptacle that my mother scoured out every evening, but some people had beautifully enamelled cans which shone white and always looked clean. I envied them.

The Hill children of Hampson farm were friends of mine; we often walked home from school together. They had a servant and a dairymaid, and for a long time it was my ambition to be the dairymaid at Hampson farm when I grew up. The dairy fascinated me. Its scrubbed stone floor, spotless, white wood shelves and benches laden with churns of cream and yellow slabs of butter spoke of a bounteous plenty which to me was out of this world. I loved to stand and watch the milk, warm from the cows, being set to cool before going through the separator, which in some miraculous way separated the golden cream from the thin, blue-white milk. I loved to see the cream poured into the churn for butter-making and to wait until the dull thud from inside the churn, turned by Mrs. Hill or the dairymaid, announced that the butter had come. But most of all I loved to see the wide-mouthed pans of milk slowly heating on the kitchen range and to watch the cream thickening on the surface. When the cream had risen and had set in a bubbly golden mass, the crocks (as we called the pans) were put to cool on the stone floor. Next day the thick crust of cream, so firm you could hold a piece in your hand, was lifted; this was the real Devon clotted cream. A wedge of cream eaten with a slice of honeycomb was a treat not easily forgotten.

The year I went to school Betty Hill taught me to milk. Betty was a little older than I and she admired my "brains". I admired her manual skills—she could sew and darn and mend as well as my mother. She also helped in the dairy, milked and made butter.

I learned to milk on Daisy, a very old and patient cow. My first attempt was a disaster. Although I pushed and pulled nothing happened, and in the end Daisy kicked over the empty bucket, and turned round and mooed at me. Several lessons later I managed the art of press and squeeze, and after that I often helped Betty and the cowman at milking-time. Sometimes I was rewarded with a mug of raw cream or a crusty slice of bread laden with cream and home-made jam.

In the summer I helped with the hay, turning it and stacking it in stooks. The thistles and grasses tore my bare legs, and the hay seeds stuck in my hair, but the smell of hay was sweet, and the June sunshine tanned my face and arms. At the end of the day we were allowed to ride back to the farm on the cart-horses which had been working in the hay field. Moonlight, the great black Shire was my favourite. He was so huge that my legs could hardly straddle him, but he moved slowly and rhythmically, and I half-sat, half-lay on his broad back, clinging to his mane with both hands. I loved the feel of his smooth, oily coat and the pungent, rich, sweaty smell of him.

Once, Betty and I found a rat's nest in a rick that was being cut down. There were five pink hairless young rats in it. Betty threw them to the ground and stamped on them; they were vermin and had to be killed.

Just beyond Hampson was another farm—Broadnymet—where the Ponsfords lived. The Hills and the Ponsfords were friends. Betty Hill would take me to Broadnymet which was built right on the edge of a moor, a desolate stretch of marsh and scrubland littered with stunted trees and outcrops of rock. Broadnymet Moor fascinated me—the silence, the strangeness, the glow and the scent of the heather in its season. The peaty streamlets ran everywhere, their beds lined with white pebbles which gleamed through the rushing waters. The moor stretched away into the far distance, and I thought it was a place where almost anything could happen.

Behind the Ponsfords' farm were the ruins of a disused church. The windows were broken, and we often climbed in, disturbing the bats which hung from the roof-beams. The place smelled musty and damp, and bird-droppings were thick on the mouldering pews, but the church gave me the same sense of awe and timelessness as did Broadnymet Moor.

The Ponsfords' farm was one of the larger farms in the neighbourhood. One of the former owners had been extremely well-to-do, with a passion for gambling. He held gambling-parties and invited friends to roister with him. Drink flowed, and the stakes were high. At one such party he mortgaged his house, his stock, his lands and his shares, and soon his wealth was gone. When his friends left, he went into his bedroom and blew his head off with a shotgun. The villagers swore that on wild winter nights his ghost could be seen galloping down the farm lane in a coach and pair, chasing after the friends who had taken his money. My grandmother told my father the story, and Dad was keen to stay up to see what there was to be seen, but when he mentioned it to Mrs. Worden, the old lady became very agitated and said, "Doan' 'ee do it cheel, doan' 'ee do it. Lie abaid." If my father ever did watch for the ghost, I never heard about it.

Although Broadnymet Moor was not as impressive as Dartmoor it was for me a magical place. One autumn evening I pestered my father to tell me about fairies, pixies and suchlike. Somehow I did not quite believe in them but I hoped they existed and I wanted my belief strengthened. My father, however, believed in an honest approach to all my problems so he told me that he did not believe in fairies, but he thought probably they were historically real in that they were survivors of a very ancient race who had lived on, after conquest, in the hills and wild places of our land. Perhaps, he said, they wore animal skins and so had been known as "furries"—if so they must have survived into historical times because the word "fur" had a Middle English root. He quoted the Cornish furry dance in support of his theory, saying that some people called it furry and some people called it fairy. I thought all this most interesting—it was much more exciting than if he had said that the dainty little butterfly folk of whom I had read in my story-books were a real possibility. Did he think there were any furries on Dartmoor or anywhere near us now, I asked. No, he did not think so. They must have all died out hundreds of years ago, but he believed there might have been pixies on Dartmoor in the times of the early tin-miners. I could hardly believe my ears. Pixies! The little folk who were always leading courting couples astray on Broadnymet Moor so that they arrived home in the small hours, to the wrath of their parents and the amusement of their neighbours. Pixies! who led farm-hands into bogs when they left the pub at nights so they did not reach home until next morning, sad and sober. I was thrilled to think there might even be a pixie somewhere around our cottage. My father pointed out that he had not said that there were pixies on Dartmoor now—but there might have been in the past. Pixies, too, he thought were the remnants of a conquered race who had gone to live in the hills. Possibly they painted their bodies with woad and were called Picti by the Romans, meaning painted men.

"But if there are no pixies now," I asked, "why do we put food out for them in our linhay?" My father answered that perhaps I had noticed we put out bread and cheese for the pixies whenever there was an escape from Dartmoor prison. Too often the escaped convict was caught on our road as he made his way towards Exeter. He said that most people who lived as we did in isolated spots made sure food was available when a man was on the run because it often saved their homes from being broken into in search of sustenance. Of course it would be wrong knowingly to help an escaped convict, but if you put out food for the pixies overnight and it was gone in the morning, who knew who had taken it?

A few weeks later on a warm October evening he suggested that we go for a walk over Broadnymet Moor. Perhaps we might see some pixies. It had been a long hot summer, and the patches of rock which littered the moor were soaked in heat so that they felt warm to the touch. The heather had faded to a dirty brown and my sandalled feet were soon thickly coated with dust and heather seeds. The moor was exciting in the half-light. Every now and then a rock in front of us would rise with a grunt and amble away, its shape changing from a block of moorstone to a sheep, cow or wild pony. Everything was strange and wonderful. In the distance Cawsand brooded darkly against the pale sky. I hopped and skipped along, stumbling over broken branches and loose rocks, splashing through rush-fringed streamlets. My father walked carefully, feeling his way with his stick.

Darkness fell quickly. Soon the moor around us was a featureless waste merging into a grey sky. Cawsand was blotted out; all the familiar landmarks were lost in the darkness. An owl hooted before setting off for a night's hunting. We saw him glide across the path a few yards ahead of us. He pounced, and there was one frightened shriek, then he was winging his way back to the hillock from which he came. I walked close to my father and held his hand.

There is a patch of marsh on Broadnymet Moor which could almost be called a bog. A wide rock basin, flooded by a small stream, is filled with mud and rotting vegetation that will one day become peat. Patches of rush and cotton-grass grow here and there on the raft of mud, twigs and reeds floating on the evil-smelling brown morass which fills the basin. Between the reeds and rushes, the marsh heaves and gurgles as the gases given off by the rotting material rise to the surface. It was a place I knew well by daylight. Once I had lost a rubber boot there; it had filled with water and slipped from my foot. On this October evening a faint, white mist hung over the marsh and the scent of decay was very strong. My father sat down on a boulder and said that if we were lucky we might see a pixie lantern. Around us the moor was dark but full of sound. Small animals scuttled through the heather, bats darted overhead and a fox called to his mate at the edge of the heathland. The air was warm and still and oppressive. The surface of the marsh gurgled and heaved, and suddenly there was a small, blue flame between the rushes. It rose and sank and flickered out only a few yards from where we were sitting. "There you are," said my father, "there's a pixie lantern for you. That's what people see on the moor and sometimes follow."

I wanted to get nearer to the place where the light had been but my father kept a firm hold of my hand. "It's marsh gas," he said. "Sometimes on warm evenings like this it ignites and you see it as a blue flame. It has helped to keep the pixie legend alive."

On the other side of the moor near Bow station there was a gipsy encampment.

The Stanleys lived there under the matriarchal rule of old Liza. Somehow, I do not remember how, I came to know them—possibly I met the children exploring Broadnymet Moor or became friendly with young Darkie out on one of his poaching expeditions. Sometimes on a Saturday I found my way to the encampment and settled myself down by one of the caravans. Liza Stanley was an old, old woman, swarthy skinned, wrinkled, dark-eyed and kind, who sat on wet days just inside the open door of her caravan, or on fine days by the communal camp fire around which the caravans were arranged. She was usually busy making clothes-pegs which the younger women peddled through the villages. She ruled the encampment with a rod of iron. It was she who allocated the jobs to be done each day; insisted that the caravans were kept brightly painted; attended the women in childbirth, arranged marriages, watched the cooking-pot, and was the financial brains of the tribe. She taught me many of her skills, such as how to skin a moorhen, how to dowse for water, how to make a kipsy—a roughly plaited twig basket holding a posy of wild flowers—how to walk a field in search of mushrooms, and the best places to look for blackberries.

Darkie Stanley was either Liza's son or her grandson, I never knew which. He was constantly in trouble with the police, and went to gaol on at least one occasion. Liza was always the prime mover behind his defence, and he owed many months of freedom to her wily brain and persuasive arguments.

Once a year the encampment was deserted. I never knew where the tribe went. One day they were all there, and next they were gone, and just as suddenly they were back again, their fire lit, their piebald ponies pulling at the grasses.

Years after I had left the village I heard that old Liza had died, and that the Stanleys had left their caravans with the brightly painted wheels, sold their ponies and gone to live in the local council houses. Several of the lads whom I had known when I was a child had fought and died in the Second World War, Darkie among them.

Recently when I was sorting through the contents of an old

trunk, I came upon the shrivelled and dried hazel fork which Liza had cut green and fresh from the hedge when she taught me to dowse.

I still think of her words when she read my hand, "A long life, a wild life, a happy life. A marriage bed, oh! what a marriage bed . . . metal on metal, wheels on wheels, but you'll die in your bed even so, my bird."

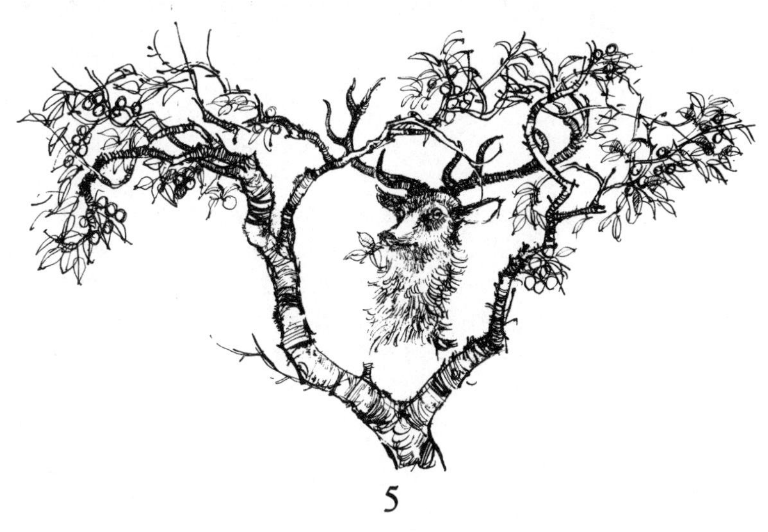

5

How we lost our damson harvest and gained a rib of venison. The fruits of the earth. A visit to Fairyland. Roast goose, Christmas pudding and bitter winter weather. The floods of early spring.

My mother did most of our gardening. Both cottages had long gardens stretching length-wise along the road from the end wall of each building. George Harris kept us well supplied with farm-yard manure which he obligingly dug in for us each autumn so that the land was very fertile. We grew all our vegetables, had a sizeable patch of raspberry canes yielding vast quantities of large, red berries, a strawberry patch that had run riot and was almost wild, gooseberry bushes, and black, red and white currants that grew in a small jungle beside the hedge. We had an apple tree which someone had thoughtfully grafted so that on one side it bore fruit for cooking and on the other side dessert apples. There was also a pear tree, two plum trees and a damson tree which was the darling of my mother's heart. Damsons were her favourite fruit, and the tree was cosseted, but in spite of this it was extremely temperamental. Most years it bore some fruit, some years it bore none at all and very occasionally it was laden with so many blue-black damsons that its lower boughs were weighed down to the ground. My mother watched the fruit ripen with a jealous eye, judging when the exact moment had come for her and myself to descend on the tree with baskets and buckets to strip it. The damsons would then be bottled for winter use or boiled on the kitchen range, and made into pots of jam to be sold in my grandmother's shop in the village.

Jam-making always began in June with gooseberry and strawberry crops; it continued until September and ended with damsons and wild blackberries. It was my job to search the store in our linhay for the last of the jam-jars and to wash and sterilize them. This was a job I hated but I loved the jam-making itself. The kitchen was warm and fragrant with the smell of boiling fruit and sugar, and soon hordes of wasps invaded us winging their way from far and near, creeping in through the open windows, and pressing through the cracks in the door frame. We put out wasp traps—jam-pots half filled with water and a spoonful of "scum" from the jam, and covered with a paper seal, pierced in one place to allow the entry of the wasp. Once the insect was inside it rarely found its way out again. Traps alone, however, could not cope with the wasps that pestered us during our jam-making and I was allowed to bring out my wooden seaside spade to bat down as many as possible.

One summer the fruit crop had been poor and my mother was relying on the damsons and the blackberries. The damson tree promised a really outstanding harvest: the fruit were large and luscious and had a healthy purple bloom. We expected to be able to make about thirty pounds of jam and borrowed extra jars from my grandmother on the strength of our anticipation. We examined the tree daily and finally decided to pick the fruit on the following Saturday morning. On the Friday the weather was fine and clear, and the moorland hills were haloed in the evening with patches of flame-bright cloud—a sure sign of fine weather to come. I went to bed early; Saturday would be a long, hard day and we were going to start picking immediately after breakfast.

I woke at dawn and ran to the window to check the weather. The ground was dry; there had been no rain to spoil the fruit. The sun rose slowly, its warmth drying the trails of mist that hung along the hedgerows. My parents were still asleep so I dressed quickly and ran to the garden. A light dew had dampened the sprout plants but they were already drying out. It was going to be a perfect day for the fruit-picking.

I made my way past the last of the runner beans, and the patch of broken earth which still held our late potatoes, to the damson tree, but before I reached it I could see that something was agitating the branches. As I drew nearer I saw the head and antlers of a huge red deer, standing on its hind legs, its forelegs pressed against the trunk. It was devouring the fruit as fast as possible, and tearing the branches of the tree into the bargain. Already the tree was almost stripped.

There was little I could do. Red deer sometimes made forays into our area, and I knew enough not to meddle with them. Usually they had been chased down from Exmoor by the hunt, and had made their way across country following the ridge of high land which joins Exmoor to Dartmoor. They were sometimes injured, usually exhausted, and always surly and evil-tempered. Often after a deer had been seen in the district there was venison to be had from one of the local farmers, as long as one asked no questions.

For a moment or two I stood appalled watching our damson crop vanish into the huge mouth. The animal saw me and kept one blood-shot eye turned in my direction while it continued to tear at the tree. Suddenly, sated, it dropped its forefeet to the ground and half leaped, half scrambled into the field through a gap in the hedge. I watched it trot downhill to the stream where it paused to drink.

At first my mother did not believe my story; then she ran to the garden to see the damage for herself. The only damsons that remained were at the very top of the tree. The ground at the foot was littered with broken branches, leaves and trampled fruit.

The following weekend Farmer Joslin sent us a rib of venison big enough to feed us for several days.

Since there were to be no damsons we had to make sure we had plenty of blackberries. We scoured the hedges round the field, filling our baskets with warm, ripe fruit. We did not bottle any fruit that year but we made blackberry and apple jam and blackberry jelly. Twenty pounds my mother took to my grandmother, to be sold in the shop; seven pounds of jam and jelly we kept for ourselves so that in the cold winter months we could taste the sweetness of summer.

That autumn we also preserved field mushrooms. I gathered basketfuls of them every morning when the sun had been on them long enough to open the buttons to pink-lined umbrellas. We wiped them carefully and strung them on twine, making a knot after each mushroom so that it was held in place about an inch from its neighbour. Then the strings were hung from the ceiling above the kitchen range where they slowly dried to brown, shrivelled knobs.

Later in the year the mushrooms could be soaked in warm water until they became plump again. They made tasty additions to stews and meat pies, and could be chopped and used in soups.

The hedgerows provided us with another source of winter food—hazel-nuts. These were gathered as soon as the green cup in which the shell was bedded had dried and turned brown. The nuts were then spread out on a tray to dry completely before being stored in boxes to be opened at Christmas. We also gathered beech-nuts, but these always seemed to give a poor return for our labour; there was so little meat in the pointed, ridged shell. A group of sweet chestnut trees in the copse off Hampson Lane provided us with food in winter. If they were roasted in the fire, the kernel came sweetly away from all its coverings. I hated the labour of freeing the nuts from the prickly green outside shell in which they were cased; I hated even more scraping the bitter brown skin from the raw kernels after the leathery shell had been torn off, so I never ate my chestnuts raw.

Christmas was a happy time. It began in early December when, muffled against the weather, we walked to Bow station and took a train to Exeter to buy presents and goodies. I took with me the store of threepenny pieces I had saved up during the year in my piggy bank. At Woolworths you could buy presents for everyone, all for threepence or sixpence—the shop did not stock anything more expensive. I bought embroidered handkerchieves for my aunts, a brooch or necklace for my grandmother, a pen for my grandfather and a pipe for my father. Mother usually bought him a tobacco-pouch to go with it. The pipe and pouch lasted him the whole year till the next Christmas. Buying a present for my mother was always difficult because she would not let me out of her sight. Usually I gave her a diary or perhaps some chocolates or a pair of artificial-silk stockings.

Shopping completed we walked up the High Street pressing through the crowds of hurrying people, and shuddering away from the edge of the pavements which seemed so very near the noisy trams rattling along the road. Always we looked for a restaurant which served steak and kidney pudding—my favourite meal. We walked over gratings above basement kitchens that leaked savoury smells; we peered at faded menus behind steamy windows—my mother carefully compared the prices. Finally we settled on a place that seemed clean and cheap and served the food we wanted. I had my steak and kidney pudding and a pile of mashed potatoes covered with rich gravy. Afterwards, I ate canned pineapple cubes and custard. The meal usually cost about three shillings a head so it was a treat to be enjoyed only once a year.

After lunch we went to Fairyland in Walton's shop. A lift decorated with cottonwool snow and tinsel icicles carried us to an upper floor where a cavernous doorway smothered in fir and holly boughs led into a marvellous complex of walks and tunnels—Fairyland itself. Here were grottoes with fountains of real water, caves with stuffed bears and wolves, green swards on which stood elves and fairies, and tableaux of story-book characters such as Snow White, Red Riding Hood, Jack the Giant-killer. We saw witch houses, ice palaces, gingerbread castles and enchanted forests, and finally, near the exit, we met Father Christmas himself seated in his sleigh. He spoke to each child, and made a note of any requests for Christmas gifts, but was careful not to promise anything unless the accompanying parent nodded to him.

After this we were decanted into the street which seemed very dark and drab after the lights of Fairyland. Through fitful sleet and rain we made our way back to Central station and caught a train for home.

In the days following our shopping expedition there were Christmas letters to write, presents to wrap and deliver, Christmas cards to paint. Cupboards were full to bursting point with Christmas food, and I was strictly forbidden to touch any of the packages under my parents' bed. We decorated the cottage with holly picked from the garden hedge, and George Harris brought us a huge bunch of mistletoe. On Christmas Eve my grandfather delivered a twelve-pound goose—his present to us. My mother made sage and onion stuffing ready for the next day.

On Christmas morning the Valor oil-heater was lit in my parents' bedroom casting its patterned glow upon the ceiling. The room was warm and the heater gave sufficient light for me to unpack the stocking and pillow-case I had found hanging at the foot of my bed. Each present was carefully unwrapped and admired, but since the gifts varied little from year to year there was no great excitement. In the stocking was a ball, a box of paints, some small oddments which my mother thought I might like, an apple, an orange, and the foot was filled with nuts. The pillow-case held one unexpected present—something I had expressed a wish for—various articles of clothing which I needed, a large box of crackers, and best of all, a book.

We ate our Christmas dinner at mid-day. My mother was up early and the goose, stuffed and surrounded by well-scrubbed apples, was soon sizzling in the oven. A large Christmas pudding boiled on top of the kitchen range beside saucepans of sprouts, carrots and potatoes. The dresser was laden with plates of nuts, grapes, oranges, dates and Jordan almonds. A large dish of scalded cream—much smoother and richer than the clotted variety—sat in the safe beside a trifle, mince pies and Christmas cake.

But Christmas was over all too soon and January, the worst month of the year according to my father, was upon us.

The moors were now covered in whiteness and barely visible against the mottled sky. Snow blurred the outlines of the garden and lay banked against the hedges. The water-bucket was frozen to the ground beside the well and had to be prized free with a chisel. At night a dog fox howled in the fields and, at first light, the crisp surface of the snow was pitted with the tracks of stoats, weasels, rats and voles. An owl from one of the elms opposite the cottages took one of Mrs. Worden's chicks, and one of our cats lost a kitten. The cottages were isolated. The road to Bow was impassable because of snow and floods. We lived on our stored food and the milk George Harris brought us from the farm.

Spring usually came in February. The weather did not improve suddenly; it thawed, froze and thawed again. Gradually the packed snow melted from the garden path and rivulets of brown water ran down the sides of the road. The little river Yeo, swollen a thousand times by the melting snow from the moors, rushed under the grey stone arch of Bow Bridge and spread over the fields beyond. The dirty swirling waters tore up bushes and trees and carried away the odd sheep or lamb. Dartmoor was still blanketed in white and the moorland roads were blocked, but gradually patches of heather showed on the sides of the tors. The snow turned to slush and the slush to water. One year an avalanche of snow fell from our thatched roof engulfing my mother who was trying to draw water from the well. She struggled free, laughing. The little stream at the bottom of the field ran full and fast tearing a bigger gap in the hedge by the cherry tree. Branches of trees, entangled with each other, made dams behind which the water built up, brown and peaty, until the dam burst with a crack and the stream surged onwards leaving a line of leaves and driftwood in the meadow.

The pale sun slanted cold rays across the land and soon there were primroses along the river bank and daffodils clustered under the trees. Catkins hung from the hazel trees like golden ribbons. The earth warmed in the spring sunlight.

In March frogs laid their spawn in the watery red mud of the ditch behind the cottage—I was forbidden to go near it. At night when a fox called, a vixen answered him.

A hedgehog was heard grunting in the garden in the evenings, and a cat had a litter of kittens. Spring had come.

6

The changing seasons. A day at the seaside. Harvest, and wild rabbits in the corn. Vizards for Hallowe'en. The year turned full circle.

The countryman's year, far more than the townsman's, is geared to the slow progress of the seasons. It was even more so in the days before farming was mechanized. Spring brought tilling of the fields which had lain dormant under the winter frosts, the sowing of seeds, lambing and the cattle freed from the shippens and farm-yards where they had been penned for easy feeding during the months when grass was sparse. Stables and cowsheds had to be cleaned of the accumulated manure, which was brought out and piled in a great heap in the farm-yard to rot and mature. Hedges had to be cut, and the branches "laid" so that they filled in any gaps. They were not entirely separated from the parent tree and consequently sprouted new upright shoots which thickened the hedge. The thinner branches were sliced off and bound into faggots to be dried and used as fuel in the following winter. Ditches were cleared of the mud and debris brought by the rains. Cottages were whitewashed and re-thatched where necessary; farm tracks were mended with blocks of moorstone. Later came sheep-shearing—usually carried out by a band of itinerant shearers who went from farm to farm. They were fast and efficient workers, and it was a pleasure to see the fleece, snowy white in its underparts, peel away from the animal's skin in one solid piece. After shearing came dipping. If there were no permanent dipping-place on the farm a four-foot hollow was dug out of the ground and lined with wood and stone. The side walls were vertical; the opposite pair shelved very gently. Wattle fences were erected to make an approach to one shelving side and an exit from the other. The hollow was filled with an orangey-red sheep dip and the sheep were driven into this between the wattle fences. When they reached the hollow they were forced to swim across. Men with wooden crooks ensured the sheep were completely engulfed by the dip, and helped any animal in difficulties. They emerged bleating indignantly, their fleeces dyed a pale rust colour but the ticks and keds which lived in their wool, and the maggots which ate into their flesh, were killed by the disinfectant. Sheep dipping was great fun.

After dipping came the hay harvest. The success of this depended largely on the farmer's weather wisdom. The grass had to be cut when it was just ripe. The horse-drawn reaper left the crop lying in swathes in the field. A willing band of helpers collected it into stooks. Rain at this point could ruin the whole crop. When it was dry the hay was collected on a sledge drawn by one of the farm horses and made into a rick. If it was still damp the heat generated as it rotted would cause spontaneous combustion and the stack would burn down.

After hay-making there was a lull of four or five weeks before the grain was ready for harvesting. Again the farmer had to pick his time carefully. Daily he would survey the fields of oats, barley and wheat where they lay golden under the summer sun. Sadly he noted the scarlet heads of poppies, the bright yellow mustard and the blue cornflowers—the weeds which had been mixed with the seed. He waited until the corn was a white-gold and the weather was set fair before he ordered the grain to be cut; then the whole work force of the farm went into the field. The reaping machine cut the grain about four inches from the ground and flung it out in straw-tied sheaves. These were collected by the farm-hands and stacked into wigwam-shaped stooks which were left to dry in the sun. If it rained heavily at this stage the stooks blackened and rotted but, if the fine weather continued, in a few days the corn was collected in a cart, and taken to a corner of the field where a threshing machine waited. This machine was usually hired, and part of the farmer's care had to be to arrange his harvest so that the corn was ready for threshing when the machine was available. The long-stemmed grain was fed into the machine by hand and there were always terrifying stories abounding of children who had caught a sleeve between the roller and had had an arm or a hand sliced off. When the threshing machine had done its work the grain was bagged up and sent to the miller to be ground into flour. The straw was made into a reed-thatched rick to be used for cattle fodder and bedding in winter.

The harvest safely in, autumn was upon us and it was time to put the rams with the ewes in order to ensure next year's crop of lambs. Turnips and swedes had to be lifted and stored in long, low piles roofed with wood or sheets of galvanized iron; the stubble had to be ploughed back into the ground and the earth sewn with winter wheat. The manure, which had been stockpiled in spring was brought out, cart-load after cart-load, and laboriously spread over the fields to be ploughed in. The cattle were brought into their winter quarters and their milk, lacking richness from the grass became thin and bluish. The year had come its full cycle.

We children had our seasons too, which interlinked with the agricultural year. In spring we were not wanted underfoot so we gathered snowdrops, primroses, daffodils and bluebells as they appeared. The schoolroom window-sills were cluttered with jam-jars of flowers and "sticky buds"—the gluey leaf-buds of the horse-chestnut. It was the season for hoops which we bowled up and down the country lanes. We went on "explorations" to see what the winter had done to our favourite haunts. Sometimes we went to see a natural curiosity such as a lamb with five legs or a calf with two heads. At Easter we gathered armfuls of blossom to decorate our homes. The first three days of May had a special significance. The first of May was courting day; we romped and laughed with the little boys and shyly held their hands. The second day of May was kissing day; we kissed in dark corners of the school and boasted blushingly about it to our friends. The third of May was stinging nettle day; every child went to school armed with a bunch of nettles with which he lashed the arms and legs of his comrades until they were covered with hot, red, itchy bumps that could only be soothed by rubbing with a green dock leaf dampened with spittle.

In June we helped in the hay-fields and made the hay "sweet" by rolling in it and giving each other a kiss. In the interval between the hay and the corn harvest we enjoyed one of the highlights of the year—the annual Sunday school outing. For the Plymouth Brethren, to which I belonged, this took place on the next to last Wednesday in July. Because our chapel was sure of divine favour we always enjoyed perfect weather. The Church of England also arranged a treat for their children which took place on the following Wednesday: they too had perfect weather.

From the end of June onwards the whole village had been preparing for its day at the seaside. Swimming-suits were unpacked from drawers where they had been stored, beach-towels were washed, sun-hats were pressed, and buckets and spades were discovered in forgotten hiding places in outhouses. Mothers cut lengths of chiffon to wind round their hats when they rode in the char-à-banc so that their millinery was anchored against the wind of passage.

The Harris children went to the Church of England outing so that Jimmy Harris was still looking forward to his trip when I was reliving mine in my imagination and describing it in detail to our cats, who were always ready to sit around and listen to one of my stories.

The last few days before the trip were almost unbearable. I was too excited to eat or sleep. When the day finally dawned I was up with the lark, making sure that my bucket and spade were safely packed in the canvas grip containing whatever we were taking with us. In the kitchen there was the mouth-watering smell of warm eggs mashed with butter to make a sandwich filling. The quarter-pound block of milk chocolate, which had lain on top of the dresser for days, was put into a paper bag with a couple of oranges. We never took anything to drink because there were plenty of tea-stalls on the beaches.

Eventually we set off, my mother clutching the grip in one hand and holding my hand with her other. In the pocket of my cotton dress was the sixpenny piece my father had given me when I kissed him goodbye.

The road to Bow village was long and dusty, and I was sure that we should arrive too late to catch the char-à-banc. I constantly urged my mother to hurry, until she threatened to turn right round and go home again if I did not keep quiet.

At last we reached the assembly point. There stood the coach, silent, waiting, surrounded by a noisy crowd of children and grown-ups. At this point my mother invariably insisted that she had left her money at home and the canvas grip had to be unpacked at the side of the road to find her purse which was securely hidden under the packet of sandwiches. We waited until our names had been ticked off on a list and then were allowed to board the vehicle and take our seats.

By now the sun had risen into the cloudless heavens. In the valley wreaths of mist still lingered beneath the trees. The moor was damson-dark, its tors silhouetted against the pale, morning sky. Everyone agreed that it was going to be a perfect day.

At last the coach roared into life and we were away. Scarves streamed in the wind, and children's hair blew into ragged tails. Boys climbed on seats to shout their delight at the passing countryside and were promptly hauled down by worried mothers. Someone sang. We all sang. The song was a tuneless expression of happiness.

The char-à-banc rumbled noisily down the country lanes through the market town of Crediton and on towards Exeter and Haldon moor. Farmlands ripe with corn and water-meadows lush with grasses gave way to the outskirts of the city. We cut through the suburbs and soon we were climbing the long ascent of Telegraph Hill. Heathclad moorland spread out before us; gorse bushes bright with blossom lined the unfenced road and, suddenly, there before us was the sea, blue as a morning speedwell, laced with diamonds of brilliant light. We fell silent at the sight and the coach sped on.

The road turned and twisted and dipped behind thickets and copses. The sea was lost, but already we could taste salt on our lips. We were approaching the town of Teignmouth. Once more we could see the sea, nearer, bluer. . . . A red cliff jutted out on our right, topped with green trees; to the west the coast shimmered in the sunshine.

The disembarkation point was near the pier and we ran to the sea-wall to look down at the sands below but our soulless parents turned away from the sea, dragging us unwillingly after them. We must go into the town and see the shops; above all we must visit Woolworths. We bought this and that to take home with us, for shopping was very limited in Bow, then, at long last, we made for the beach and found a dry place against the sea-wall where we settled down. Nearer the sea the sand was dark and wet and littered with shining shells, the legs of green crabs and bundles of papery whelk eggs. I was shrouded in the beach towel while I shed my dress and put on my swim-suit. It was buttercup yellow so that I could be easily seen and had a high neck, short sleeves, and legs hidden under a brief skirt. My sandals were wrapped in my dress, and placed tidily in the grip, and then I was off to the water's edge.

The sand was coarse and cold beneath my feet. I looked back; already my mother seemed a long way away. The sea stretched before me, vast, endless. Ripples of cool water played around my toes and crept over my ankles. I stepped forward and was knee-deep. Around me other children paddled, clutching buckets and spades, and a few intrepid spirits lay on their backs, lashing the water with their heels. Mothers with skirts pinned up to their knees stood watching. Suddenly, I felt small and frightened. I ran back across the sand, and flung myself down by our bag of food. Already I was hungry.

The morning seemed endless. By noon the beach was packed. The sand, dried by the sun, was scorchingly hot so that it was painful to walk on with bare feet. My arms and legs were soon burned red and I frequently rushed into the sea to cool off. At last the sandwiches were unpacked. They were gritty with sand but tasted delicious. The bar of chocolate, melted to a warm "goo", was licked from its silver paper wrapping. Wasps attracted by the smell of sugar were beaten off with sticky fingers. My mother said that it was unsafe to bathe for at least an hour after food so, having washed my face and hands in the sea, I settled down to make sandcastles. Other children joined me and soon we had a complicated system of fortifications spread across the beach: moats were filled with slopping buckets of water from the sea. We went deeper and deeper each time before plunging our buckets into the waves. Soon, all pretence abandoned, we were "swimming" with one foot still on the bottom or floating, hair awash, under the summer sun.

The day passed all too quickly. By tea-time, when I ate my orange and a strawberry ice-cream, the tide was already lapping at the battered remains of our sandcastle. We rebuilt the walls and tried to channel the water into the moats, but the fortifications crumbled under the assault of the waves; the castle was doomed.

A cool breeze sprang up as the sun sank into the western sky. The pier cast long dark shadows on the sand, and the sea became grey and menacing. It was time to go home.

I was dusted and towelled free of sand, and my cotton dress was popped over my head. I slipped off my wet swim-suit, and rinsed it clean in the sea. The water felt cold; green strands of sea-weed clung to my ankles.

The char-à-banc was waiting by the pier. If we had any money left, we slipped a penny into the machines which dispensed small bars of chocolate before boarding the coach. We were quiet on the way home; we were tired and there was so much to remember. From the top of Haldon Hill we looked back to the sea—a grey line on the horizon.

In Crediton we stopped to buy fish and chips, and spent the rest of the journey home eating them, with greasy fingers, from their newspaper wrapping. The walk back to our cottage was almost done in my sleep. I did not remember going to bed.

For several weeks after the Sunday school outing I relived my marvellous day. I sat in the garden and told the cats all that I had seen and done. Attracted by my voice and flattered by the attention which I showed them, they sat round me or rubbed against my arms and legs with every appearance of intelligent understanding. I elaborated on my adventures and they grew more and more incredible as the days passed. Soon I realized that story-telling was almost as good as the real thing—I could recreate my enjoyment as I wished. I tried some of my stories out on my parents and was promptly in trouble for telling lies.

August came and went. The reaping machines rumbled past our cottage on their way to the harvest fields. We children went to see the grain cut. Round and round went the machine and the field of golden wheat shrank to a square, then to a narrow oblong surrounded by stubble which scratched our legs. The men waited with their ash sticks, dogs quiet at their feet. As the last few swathes were cut, the rabbits which had been driven to the centre of the field by the noise of the reaper, ran out. Men and dogs fell on them; few escaped. A pile of grey-brown twitching bodies grew by the gate.

When the reaping was finished the rabbits were shared out among the helpers. Sometimes I was offered one to take home but I always refused it. I could not bear the feel of the soft, warm fur.

The end of the August holidays was virtually the end of summer. We went back to school taking with us our skipping-ropes, for skipping was the autumn game. Champions of the art could skip forwards and backwards, crossing and uncrossing their hands. Groups of girls in the playground twirled a rope in pairs while others ran through or jumped "Salt, mustard, vinegar, pepper", the tempo increasing with the name of each condiment.

Early in September there was always one day on which school attendance dropped almost to zero because most of the children were away to Broadnymet Moor picking blackberries and "'urts" as we called the wortleberries. These small blue-black berries grew on low bushes all over the moor and made excellent tarts and pies although they were not very good for bottling or jam-making. In the days of my mother's childhood they had been even more plentiful and the school had closed down on "'urts day". Mr. Pyne, however, disapproved of this practice and would not grant us the holiday.

The evenings grew darker, and the mornings were crisp with frost. The devil came and spat on the blackberries and made them unfit to eat.

Hallowe'en was celebrated by the making of masks, which we called vizards, and turnip lamps. For the latter, a fresh turnip was hollowed out with a kitchen knife, and holes were cut in its outer layer to resemble eyes and mouth. A candle was lit and placed inside and the "head" was put in the window. Seen before a darkened room the effect was quite ghostly.

We played games to see whom we should marry, but the boys took no part in this.

Soon after Hallowe'en came Bonfire Night. Fireworks were too expensive for most families, but nearly everyone had a bonfire in their back garden where they baked potatoes and charred lumps of dough on the end of sticks. The Harrises and I usually had a few sparklers (six for a penny), rip-raps (a farthing each), Catherine wheels—very expensive at a halfpenny each—and several boxes of coloured matches. One year we had a Roman Candle, and a rocket which soared into the sky before ending as a puff of smoke.

November swept the last of the leaves from the trees. We came home from school, our cheeks reddened by wind, our fingers blue with cold. In the fields we saw the rams covering the ewes, and speculated knowledgeably on the number of lambs each farmer would have. The end of the month brought flurries of snow down from the moor, and Cawsand Beacon was mantled in white. One night, looking from my bedroom window, I saw a vixen crossing the field, her nose to the ground: three cubs followed. I told no one. George Harris would have shot them as a menace to their chickens.

December came in with a bitter wind blowing down from the hills. The smoke from our kitchen range came back down the chimney, and each morning the garden was white with hoar frost. When I went to bed, the oil-heater was lit in my bedroom so that I could undress in the warm. I lay in bed and watched the patterns cast on the ceiling by its perforated top, and thought about Christmas.

7

The miller's son and the wheelwright's daughter. A Victorian lady who ran a grocery business and reared seven children. Two old Devon farm-houses, and the village girl who went abroad to seek her fortune.

My mother had many relatives in the surrounding villages. Her father, Robert Riddaway, came from a line of farmers who had lived in Devon since before the Norman Conquest. The Reddaways were mentioned in the Domesday Book as tenant farmers holding Redway Farm at Sandford Courtenay. The line had stretched unbroken from father to son right down to the twentieth century. Younger sons, whom the farm could not support, had gone out to seek their fortunes and to settle all over Devon. My great-great-grandfather, who had little schooling and could not spell, had set out from the little farm huddled under the Dartmoor hills to become a miller at Brushford in mid-Devon. It was at Brushford Mill in the mid-nineteenth century that my grandfather had been born and entered in the church register as Robert Riddaway. He had grown up and left the mill which later passed out of family hands, and had taken a job as a farm-hand in Coleridge. There he had met Fanny Blackmore, the daughter of a wheelwright. Fanny was a year or two older than Robert and, in country eyes, a little above his station. She was one of a large family, and kept house for her father, since her mother was dead. John Blackmore, her father, had formerly lived at Chittlehampton in North Devon near the Exmoor hills from which his family came. He had possessed the gift of healing, and so many sick people came to him from all over the county that, worn out and unable to pursue his trade, he had left Chittlehampton to hide himself in Coleridge. There he once more set up as a wheelwright, succeeding to the extent that he sent his youngest son, George to Cambridge University.

The Blackmores bitterly opposed the marriage of Fanny and Robert Riddaway, but Fanny was determined. Between them, she and Robert raised enough money to start a shop. They had left Coleridge, married, and moved to Bow where they bought premises in the centre of the village, and stocked it with groceries, dried cod, shoes, millinery and cotton goods. The shop was opened in 1888, and in the same year their first child, my mother, was born. Because of its connection with the cotton trade the shop was called Manchester House.

The living quarters were old, probably dating from the seventeenth century. Tradition says that Charles I slept there in 1644 when he passed through the village in pursuit of the Earl of Essex. At that time the building was an alehouse. The original entrance, an arched doorway, and a cobbled passage leading through the house to the stableyard still remained. The parlour and bedrooms were on the right of the passage, the kitchen on the left. My grandfather had the shop built on to the side of the kitchen from which it could be reached internally by means of a flight of steps.

Fanny who was the brains behind the project, continued to expand the business, and in the next ten years had built up a concern which employed several local women. She also produced seven more children of whom only one died in infancy.

It was Fanny who made and decorated the hats for the millinery shelves and who organized the rounds made by my grandfather to the surrounding villages in his pony and trap. She prepared the grocery orders he took with him, and checked the poultry, butter and eggs he brought back. From Eggesford in the Taw valley to Hittisleigh near the upper Teign every cottage and farm bought their supplies from Riddaway's stores, often paying with their own surplus produce. On Fridays my grandfather set off with a load of poultry, eggs, cream and honey for Exeter market where he rented a stall. My grandmother stayed up all night plucking chickens and packing butter—only when Nellie, the pony, and the trap had vanished up the road could she relax and set about her household chores.

My grandfather came back very late, and as soon as Nellie's hooves were heard on the cobbles outside the shop, Granny dropped everything and helped to stow the cart in its shed across the road and stable the pony. While my grandfather fed Nellie she laid a cloth on the end of the scrubbed pine table in the kitchen for her husband's supper, setting before him a huge steak and kidney pie or a stew followed by a heaped plate of apple pie and cream, or jam tart and custard, and tea so strong and sweet that the spoon almost stood up in it. Grandad called weak tea "tatie-water".

The soft down from the birds Granny had plucked the night before was sold as filling for mattresses and pillows. The children as they grew up were responsible for packing feathers into sacks. They also took the chicken entrails to bury in the garden.

The goods sold well in Exeter market and my grandfather often had his pockets stuffed with pound notes. Unfortunately he was careless with money when left to his own devices and by the time he left Exeter he would have parted with a good half of his profits. As the years passed my grandmother became less patient with her husband's spendthrift ways.

Granny looked a frail and gentle woman. She was small, with delicate bones, a slender figure and an oval face topped by a mass of soft curly hair. She had, however, a will of iron. Before her marriage she had been a staunch member of the Church of England. Robert Riddaway had been brought up as a Plymouth Brother. After her marriage, determined to share every aspect of her husband's life, Fanny had become a member of Robert's chapel, and within a few years she was the strictest of Plymouth Sisters while Robert, never a very ardent chapel-goer, had ceased to attend at all. She therefore had a two-fold whip with which to flay his careless habits—her need of every penny for her growing family, and the hatred with which the chapel regarded intemperance and wastefulness. She was conscious too, that her brothers and sisters who visited her occasionally, talked among themselves about the way poor Fanny was having to cope. The marriage was turning out just as the family had said it would.

But in spite of all this Granny adored her husband.

I never met any of her sisters, although there was constant talk between my mother and her sisters about Aunt Kezia who was housekeeper to the Chichesters of Arlington Court in North Devon, but I did know several of my grandmother's brothers.

Great-Uncle George, Granny's youngest brother, was headmaster of a school in Plymouth. He was sober, kind and erudite as became a head-teacher. His wife, Great-Aunt Helen, was an expert Honiton lace-maker who made altar cloths for use in Exeter Cathedral.

Another brother of my grandmother was Great-Uncle Joe who had been employed as a clerk by the Southern Railway Company. In those days this was a very good job and Joe retired early with a healthy bank balance. After a year or two of boredom, he bought a farm, Nichol's Nymet, halfway between Bow and North Tawton and settled down there with his housekeeper, Rosie, whom he eventually married. She and her daughter and grandchildren filled his life.

Joe, too, visited his sister Fanny now and then, and I think that my grandmother was really fonder of him than she was of her brother George, but George commanded greater respect because he was a Master of Arts.

I remember Great-Uncle Joe chiefly because he had two railway coaches in his garden, and in these I used to play trains.

Granny's eldest brother, John Blackmore, had a farm called Tucking Mill at Zeal Monachorum. Great-Uncle John, when I knew him, was an old, old, man with a long, white beard, who spent his days sitting in the ingle-nook fire-place. His daughter, my mother's cousin Blanche, married a man from Brixham, Harold Carnell, and they, with the help of Blanche's older brother, "Willumenry", ran the farm.

Tucking Mill, as the name suggests, was an old wool-cleaning or fulling mill. The water-wheel which had powered the fulling process still remained in front of the house and the mill-leat ran alongside the yard. The house itself, a long low seventeenth-century building, fascinated me. The rooms seemed so large after our cottage; the oak beams were dark, low and heavy; the fire-place, with its assortment of hooks coming down the chimney, was vast. The hearth held a wood fire summer and winter. A whole tree trunk was dragged into the kitchen and its end pushed into the blaze. As it burned away the trunk was pushed farther and farther across the floor until the whole was consumed.

A small oven in the wall beside the fire-place was heated by wood faggots which were thrust into it and then set alight. When the flames had died down, meat, cakes, bread and delicious egg and milk custards were cooked in the embers. Everything had a slightly smoky taste but this improved the flavour.

Tea-time at Tucking Mill was a delight. The table laden with home-made bread, scones, jam and cakes, stewed fruits and custard, always bore a large bowl containing about a quart of scalded cream. This was cream which had been separated from the milk in the usual way and then scalded over the fire in a large pan set inside another pan filled with water. It differed from clotted cream in that the whole milk was used to make the latter which was drier, thicker and lumpier. Scalded cream was an incomparably smooth, smoky, delicious delicacy which the family ate freely. We rarely stayed for supper at Tucking Mill since it was rather a long way to go home afterwards, but on the few occasions we did, we were served with enormous platters of home-cured ham, wedges of cheese, hunks of bread and pints of sweet cider. Great-Uncle John in his ingle-nook mumbled away at his food with toothless gums all day long. He took so long over each meal that no sooner had he finished one than the next was ready.

When I was six years old Cousin "Willumenry" had given me a little pig to keep. It was the runt of the litter and very, very small. I hugged its pink, hairless body to my chest and ran to show it to my mother. Permission to keep it was instantly refused. My parents had no idea how to look after a pig and doubted, in any case, if it would live. I burst into tears and the piglet started to squeal in sympathy. Eventually I was persuaded to return the animal to the straw beside its mother and "Willumenry" drove us all home in a trap pulled by Ginger, the bright chestnut pony. My mother scolded him roundly for making such a thoughtless gift.

The Blackmores were a remarkable family. Many of them had

marked artistic gifts, and another time and place might well have brought them fame and prosperity. They traced their descent from a John Blackmore who had been awarded in the seventeenth century a grant of land on Exmoor. Craftsmen rather than farmers, they were wood-carvers, wheelwrights, potters and weavers. The writer, Richard Dodridge Blackmore, was of their stock. The fine-boned Blackmore face was a family characteristic. The broad, high forehead, deep-set blue eyes with high cheek-bones and wide mouth were unmistakable. Uncle George once told me that the name Blackmore came from "blackamoor" as applied by the natives of Devon to the survivors of the Spanish Armada who were shipwrecked in North Devon. It may be so for the sallow skin, dark hair and the bone structure of the family could well be Spanish in origin.

The Riddaways, on the other hand, were typical moor-folk with their stocky, sturdy frames, ruddy faces, brown eyes and hair. They lacked the fire and the will of the Blackmores but made up for this by a slow, patient approach to the problems of life. Centuries of wresting a living from the harsh soil of the hills had taught them to expect disappointments and disasters and to ride these out with equanimity.

Great-Uncle Tom Riddaway, the only one of my grandfather's brothers whom I knew, had a farm called Falkedon at Spreyton. It was an old farm-house of the kind known as a "long house". The cow-sheds which had once adjoined the kitchen had been made into a parlour. In the kitchen itself was an enormous open hearth. Great-Uncle Tom and Great-Aunt Jane, who was almost blind, lived there with their two sons, Harold and Jack, and daughter Rosalind. Another daughter, Clarrie, was a teacher somewhere in North Devon.

The Blackmore blood in my mother had made her determined to get something more out of life than Bow could offer. The Riddaway blood had given her the patience to equip herself for the outside world. The bright girl of Bow school, she had worked in her spare time as a domestic help to the head-master's family, and had received in return, not money, but extra lessons. After three or four years as a pupil–teacher in the school, she had left at the age of fifteen years and had gone to seek her fortune in London, securing for herself a post as a children's nurse. The family for whom she worked had connections in France, and eventually my mother had gone to work there, taking a post with the family of the Duchess of Guiche. She quickly became fluent in French and was regarded as a treasure by her employers. Recommended from family to family she worked in Italy, Spain and Germany, learning each language in turn and progressing from nurse to governess. Her proudest possession was a crystal fob watch given her by Crown Prince Wilhelm of Germany. Anecdotes about the peculiarities of the families of the Royal Houses of Europe often crept into her conversation so that I grew up with a very intimate knowledge of upper-class society in the early twentieth century.

In 1915 she returned from Germany (where she had been briefly interned) to England and took a job with the Air Inspection Department in London. It was while she was working there in 1916 that she met my father, George Lane, a Londoner whose origins remained for me shrouded in mystery. I never knew my grandparents nor my paternal aunts and uncles, and my father never spoke of them. All I knew was that Dad had been invalided out of the army, and that for the sake of the little health that remained to him my parents had moved to Devon where I was born.

8

Church and chapel-goers. "Though our sins were as scarlet. . . ." Baptism in the river. Church socials and village fêtes.

Bow church is situated some distance from the village in the hamlet of Nymet Tracey which was the original settlement. It was not until the latter part of the twelfth century that Bow sprang up beside the main road as the result of a market charter granted to a member of the de Tracey family. It took its name from the bow-shaped stone bridge spanning the river Yeo.

Before the advent of motor transport the worshippers could be seen each Sunday morning and evening, streaming out from the village, past the school, past the village hut, past Hubbard's nurseries, past the football ground, through Kittiwells to the church of St. Bartholomew. On a wet and blustery day it needed some devotion to make the trip because, unless a much longer walk was taken along the hard road, the short cut through Kittiwells followed a path that was nothing more than a muddy track awash with rainwater and slippery with loose clay.

Kittiwells was a marsh in summer and little more than a bog in winter. The raised track ran between clumps of rushes interspersed with pools of stagnant water. In the driest of summers it was not possible to cross the marsh other than by the path, although we children spent many happy hours trying to do that very thing. We ended up wet and muddy to the knees, and rather smelly.

From the turnstile by the road the path ran gently downhill to where a culvert carried a stream under it. Here there were clumps of reeds and bulrushes and tall feathery fronds of sedge. In spring the stream was lined with kingcups and ladies' smocks. It was always surprising to see the water running clear and sparkling over its bed of stones; everywhere else in Kittiwells it was oily with blue clay and slimy with rotten leaves. From the culvert, the track went uphill to another stile locally known as a kissing-gate.The marsh was now left behind and the path ran beside a hedge through a pasture field which in winter was wet and muddy, but in spring and summer was bright with buttercups and daisies. The hedge was a Devon bank topped with holly bushes and hazels, its lower parts dotted with dog violets and primroses in the early part of the year and later glowing with the pink flowers of herb robert and campion. In May and June, where the vegetation was sparse, tiny brown and green lizards lay warming themselves in the sun. In July and August the bank was covered with wild strawberries. In autumn the brambles and trees at the top of the hedge were heavy with luscious blackberries and sweet, juicy hazel-nuts. From the pasture field the path led out on to the road and it was only a short distance to Nymet Tracey church.

As a child I never attended a service in the church because being a member of the Plymouth Brethren I equated church-going with the black mass and devil worship. Those members of the Church of England whom I knew well, I thought were misguided to say the least, and rather stupid not to realize the perils to which they were subjecting their immortal souls. But I sometimes went into the empty church with two friends of mine, Isobel and Gladys Pickard, who lived in a nearby farm. The dim interior filled me with awe, not because of its sanctity or its architectural beauty, but simply because tradition had it that the church was built by William de Tracey—one of the murderers of Thomas à Beckett—in expiation of his sin. It is interesting that de Tracey chose to build the church in a nymet, or wood sacred to pagan customs. Was it his way of renouncing a pre-Christian religion? I did not think on these lines when I was a child but the link between the building and à Beckett of whom I had read so much, fascinated me.

Religion played a very important part in our lives in the 1920's. The whole of Bow village was divided into two camps—the Church of England and the Non-Conformists. The latter consisted of the Congregationalists and the Plymouth Brethren. The rector was regarded as one of the gentry—he owned a horse and trap and kept a maid of all work and a cook. The Rectory, near the church, was a fine and imposing building. The Congregational minister came a little lower down the social scale but was still regarded with considerable respect. He lived in the Manse, near the school, and maintained a social standing slightly above that of the general run of the villagers. The Plymouth Brethren were led by a body of elders of whom Mr. and Mrs. Panting were the seniors. They lived in the chapel house and were looked up to for their piety rather than their social position. My parents were somewhat unwilling members of the chapel flock; in fact my father would not go to the services because the Brethren disapproved of his habits of smoking and drinking, but my aunts and my grandmother were pillars of the chapel, so for reasons of family solidarity my mother went to chapel every Sunday and I went to Sunday school.

Each summer the village was visited by an evangelist who came to reawaken enthusiasm in those who were already committed to the Plymouth Brethren way of life and to convert as many as possible of those who still lived in darkness. A marquee was set up in the meadows by the river and daily meetings were held there in the afternoons and evenings for a whole week. Seated on wooden benches, sweating under the hot canvas, we children attended the afternoon sessions. We scuffed our toes in the cool grass so that it gave off a sharp smell to help combat the stuffiness of the tent. The evangelist harangued us about our sins, painted alarming word-pictures of hell-fire and pleaded with us "to let Jesus enter our hearts". The tenor of the meetings was highly emotional. The preacher himself was invariably a young man and possessed an attractive personality. He used his voice magically, hypnotically, inspiring in us a religious fervour of which we had never imagined ourselves capable. His assistant coaxed harmony from an ancient piano and the preacher sang. . . . Heavens! how those evangelists could sing! And then he prayed and we went down on our knees and cried out that we were saved. Hallelujah! We were saved. We were washed in the blood of the Lamb.

At the door of the tent the preacher shook hands with us as we went out blinking into the sunshine. Outside we avoided each other's eyes, shamefacedly kicked at tufts of grass and returned to our sinful ways.

A child who attended all the sessions received at the end a gilt medallion, inscribed with a biblical text, as a memento. I collected several such medallions.

At the end of the week the marquee was taken down, the wooden benches disappeared, and the evangelist, his assistant and the piano vanished overnight. All that remained was a patch of yellow, trampled grass in the meadow by the river.

The grown-ups were as susceptible to the persuasions of the evangelists as we were, but their conversions usually lasted longer. Often the adults who were saved from the hell-fire became staunch members of the chapel and abjured their former habits of smoking, drinking and hell-raising. Sometimes the preacher captured a few souls from the Congregationalist or even the Church of England and then there was much rejoicing in the chapel community. One summer, a band of itinerant players were in the village and the leading lady was converted and settled down in the village, marrying a local lad.

In late summer outdoor baptismal services were held for those who had been converted during the year. The ceremony took place in the little river Yeo at a spot where gently sloping banks led into a deep pool. The congregation assembled by the river's edge, prayers were said and hymns were sung; then the leading elder, his trousers tucked into thigh boots, strode into the water. The folk to be baptized were led out to him, the men in their oldest suits, the women decently clad in long dresses weighted at the hem with small stones. The elder supported the head of the initiate in his right hand and used his left to deftly plunge him into the water until he was completely submerged. The baptismal text was said rather hurriedly and then the half-drowned celebrant was hauled to his feet and handed back to friends on the river bank. It was considered irreverent to splutter, cough or show any signs of distress so a large bath-towel was quickly thrown over the head of the new brother and his body was swathed in blankets. Quavering "Hallelujahs" could be heard beneath the wrappings as he stumbled home to change his clothes.

The ceremony was always arranged some weeks ahead and no change in the weather ever admitted its cancellation. The waters of the Yeo coming straight down from the moor were cold even in the hottest summer and on a chilly, windy day the ducking must have been quite unpleasant, yet no one ever seemed to be physically the worse for their baptism.

The other denominations did not seem to go in for evangelists or outdoor baptisms, relying for their excitements on missionaries from darkest Africa and church socials. The latter were held in the village hut and were regarded as wicked orgies by the older members of the Brethren. I cannot imagine how it came about but I certainly went to several church socials and thoroughly enjoyed them. The evening began with youngsters and adults sitting on schoolroom chairs around a floor as slippery as an ice-rink. We all wore our best finery, artificial silk stockings and sleeveless dresses; my hair was always in ringlets having been curled overnight in damp rags, though as the evening progressed, they lost their shape and my hair fell as straight as ever.

Proceedings opened with a game calculated to break down our shyness—something like "Truckle-The-Trencher", in which a round dish was spun in the centre of the floor, the spinner called a number and the watcher who had been allocated that number rushed to catch the dish before it collapsed. The secret was to delay calling until the trencher began to wobble. The watcher then had to make a mad dash across the slippery floor usually skidding up, in a flurry of skirts if the player was a girl, as the plate fell flat. He or she then had to pay a forfeit. The whole game, played with skill and malice, was an excellent way of getting even with one's enemies.

After "Truckle-The-Trencher" we danced "A Hunting We Will Go", "Poor Jack Went A'Courting", or "Here We Come Gathering Nuts In May". These were more restful pastimes. The entertainment that followed was varied. Sometimes there were pencil and paper games, or making fancy hats from newspapers, the excitement of "Musical Chairs", or "Passing the Parcel". Towards the end of the evening we always played "Postman's Knock" which the lads had been calling for ever since the games began. This was a game for the adolescents but we children took part. Sheepishly we called our boyfriends out for one parcel and two letters (a hug and two kisses) in the darkness of the veranda outside the hut. We went back into the room giggling and red-faced.

"Postman's Knock" was followed by dancing. We children did not participate, and sat self-conscious and tired on the seats around the floor while our elders gyrated in each other's arms doing a slow foxtrot, a waltz or a quickstep to the music of a gramophone.

The evening ended about eleven when we spilled out into the cool darkness to find our way home. Bicycles were pulled from the space under the hut and carbide lamps cast a wavering light on the roads. Those of us who were on foot went off arms linked singing "Horsey Keep Your Tail Up", or "I'm Forever Blowing Bubbles".

The afternoon equivalent of a church social was a village fête. Fêtes were held in the football field two or three times a year for various causes which needed to raise money.

The entrance to a fête was free but a man at the gate sold tickets which bore "lucky" numbers, though it was not obligatory to buy these. Inside the field, tents and wooden booths had sprung up all over the place. There were white elephant stalls where unwanted household goods and furniture were on sale, jam, preserves and cake stalls, sweets, ice-cream and mineral waters, hoop-la and bran dips (a barrel filled with bran from which for a penny you could pull out a present). Somewhere in the centre of the field was an enclosure where a squealing young pig was tied to a stake by its back leg. For threepence you guessed the weight of the pig—the winner taking the animal home at the end of the day. For another threepence in the next enclosure you attempted to catch a greased pig in your arms and put it in a basket. If you succeeded in doing this you won ten shillings. In the corner of the field was a patch of ground laid out for the buried treasure competition. Here for twopence you planted a wooden peg bearing your name and address. The nearest peg to the pre-arranged site of the treasure won the prize.

The villagers came in crowds and spent the afternoon wandering between the tents eating ice-cream, tiger nuts or rubbery pink strips of jellied almonds. Strangers from as far afield as Copplestone and Crediton vied with the locals in tests of skill. The village band played in the background pausing now and then to drink long draughts of home-made lemonade. We children sucked farthing gob-stoppers, brandished sherbert fountains, or bought lemonade powder which we licked from the palms of our hands.

Towards the end of the afternoon the tea-tent began to bulge at its sides, and peeping under the canvas, we could see the long tables set with splits and cream, raspberry buns, fruit salad and fairy cakes covered with icing and sprinkled with "hundreds and thousands". Strong, sweet tea was dispensed from urns that hissed steam every time the taps were turned. After tea the stalls which had sold out were dismantled, the winners of the competitions were announced, prizes presented and a space cleared in the centre of the field for a wrestling match. Hefty young men sweated and strained together to prove their skill. Kegs of cider were produced from cool places in the hedgerows and the fun grew faster and more furious. Children and women went home.

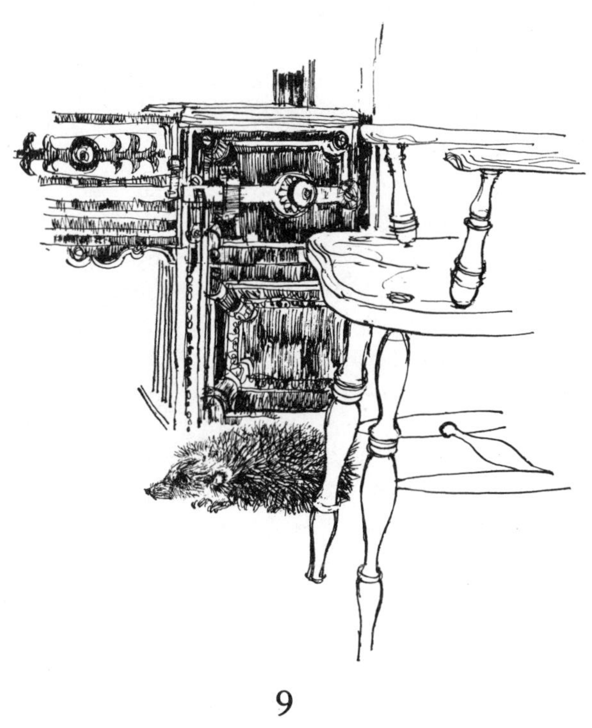

9

Of chickens, cats, rats and hedgehogs. A snake in the jam-jar. Wild life of fields, woods and water-meadows. The price of a moleskin coat.

It was inevitable that as a country child I should have a lot to do with animals. The life I lived, more out of doors than in, taught me to accept the parallel existence of the animal world. I saw the farm animals—the great Shire horses used for ploughing and reaping, the cows which gave us milk, the sheep that provided us with wool, the goats, pigs, hens, ducks and geese roaming loose in the farmyards—as friends who provided us with food and comfort. I did not dwell too closely on the fact that the hog's pudding I greatly enjoyed may have been made from the intestines of Whacky, a pig whom I knew so well that he came to my whistle, nor that our Christmas goose might be a bird which I had teased since it was a gosling. These things were a necessary and normal part of life: the animals had their lives as we had ours. Their end came at the appointed time and must be accepted. Unnecessary death or suffering, however, was another matter. I cried bitterly when the fluffy yellow chicks, newly hatched by Mrs. Worden's hens, were taken by rats. I grieved when one of our cats died, or a kitten was killed in an accident. I was doubtful about the killing of the rabbits in the harvest fields, and I hated to see any animal wantonly injured.

The fields and woods were full of wild life. Because the animals suffered no harm from us they were comparatively fearless. A family of hedgehogs lived in our garden and fed regularly from our cats' dishes. They ran freely in and out of the open cottage door. In spring and autumn they warmed themselves on the kitchen range before being dislodged by my mother, who complained that they were alive with fleas. They were, but since the cats and dogs and all the rest of us had fleas, I thought it was an unnecessary quibble.

The cats and the hedgehogs were constantly at war with the rats which lived in George Harris's wood-stack. These rats lived well on the grain Mrs. Worden scattered on the ground for her hens. They also took eggs and the odd newly hatched chick.

An uneasy truce existed between the cats and the hens broken by occasional lapses on the part of the cats. It was commonplace to see our cats sitting washing themselves in the chicken run ignoring the birds which scratched in the earth around them. In the evenings the cats were often joined by the hedgehogs who burrowed their way in under the wire netting. When dusk had fallen and the birds had settled down for the night, the hedgehogs rooted for scraps of food in the run, while the cats prowled ceaselessly round the wood-stack.

The rats, however, treated both cats and hedgehogs with contempt. On hot afternoons, when the cats were dozing and the hens were somnolent, they would slink into the run to pick up grain, and then would sit preening themselves until the cats awoke. They were enormous creatures as big, if not bigger than the cats, with glossy brown coats which shone in the sunshine. Their beady black eyes watched closely every movement of their enemies but often cats, rats and hens sunned themselves together for quite a long while before a hen came awake with a frightened squawk which sent the other birds fluttering and crying on to the roof of their hut and woke the cats to their business.

The rats, combing their whiskers with their forepaws, affected to ignore the turmoil but in reality they held every sleek muscle tensed for action. It was not until a stalking cat crouched to pounce that the rat would turn to face its enemy. If the cat was young and inexperienced, it lunged forward excitedly and missed its target. A bloody battle then followed in which the rat was attacked from all sides by several cats, but even then the outcome was far from certain. Sometimes the cats were victorious, crowding the rat until one of them could leap on its back and inflict a killing bite into the spinal cord just above the shoulders. Other times a cat, its face streaming blood, retreated to the safety of the wood-stack, shouldering aside rats right and left as it moved, and occasionally a cat would be seized by the throat and its jugular artery severed by the rat's sharp teeth before it was flung aside to die in a pool of blood.

The hedgehogs on the whole did better than the cats since they could curl up and present an impenetrable barrage of spines to the rat's attack; but they rarely succeeded in killing a rat unless it was very young.

For some reason cats and hedgehogs never joined forces to fight the common enemy.

Both hedgehogs and cats also fought with snakes. The hedgehogs killed and ate them; the cats dragged them home and left them dying in the garden.

One summer I had a pet grass snake—a beautiful creature marked with green and black like an adder—which I kept in a lidded two-pound jam-jar on an outside window-ledge. Much of my time was spent in catching flies and young frogs to feed it. It seemed quite tame and made no attempt to wriggle away when I took it out of the pot and sat with it on my lap. Its skin was soft and smooth and warm to the touch. Holding it was like holding a skein of silk. When autumn came I was afraid that it might die of cold in the jam-jar so I set it free in the garden hedge. It slithered under some dead leaves and I never saw it again.

There were badgers, stoats and weasels in the hedges of the fields behind our cottage and once I saw a weasel leading her young along a dry ditch. The three kits gambolled along beside their mother, their eyes bright and their coats shining in the sunlight. At intervals the bitch stopped and scolded them—"tch, tch, tch"—or batted the nearest one with her paw so that for a moment they trotted along in more seemly fashion. She curled her upper lip when she saw me and led them into the hedge.

A badger family lived in a sett beneath the roots of an elm tree at the top of the field, but I only once saw the clubs playing outside. It was a sunny afternoon and they rolled over and over among the buttercups and ox-eye daisies, tumbling over each other like outsize kittens. Then suddenly they vanished, sliding down the hole beneath the tree. My father said that I was lucky to have seen them as it was most unusual for them to venture out in daylight. I clamoured to stay up to see them after dark but the summer evenings were too long and I was sent to bed before dusk.

There were otters along the banks of the little river Yeo, and otter holts on Broadnymet Moor. Once a year there was an otter hunt. Men on foot came with dogs to seek out the animals which were supposed to ruin the trout and salmon fishing. When an otter was sighted the hunt followed the hounds along the river bank, often going miles across country right up to the foot-hills of Dartmoor. So wily was their prey that it doubled back and forth across the river, dodged through impenetrable patches of brambles, or swam through deep water so that its scent vanished. Quite often the hounds lost the trail and no kill was made.

On sunny afternoons it was possible to watch families of otters sporting in the deep pools of the river. The mother kept watch from a vantage point on a log or rock while the cubs dived and played in the water. Every now and then she would swim with them, often finding an eel or a small roach with which to tease them. The cubs swam after her as she turned and twisted, holding the fish crosswise in her mouth. Then, tiring of the game, she flipped the fish high into the air and swam back to the water's edge while the cubs scrambled and fought for the delicacy.

It was pleasant to lie in the grass by the water-side to watch them. There was no other sound than the splashing of the cubs at play and the drowsy hum of the honey bees as they visited the buttercups and daisies growing thickly on the river bank. If you lay relaxed and very still and did not twitch as the giant gold and black dragonflies zoomed by, brushing your face with their wings, nor moved sharply to swat a mosquito which was sinking its teeth into your flesh, you seemed to become part of the essential life of the river bank. Identity floated away; the warmth of the sun melted your shape into the cool earth. You vibrated with the joy of the humble-bee on the clover flowers, felt the coldness of the river-bed with the diving cubs, exhilarated in the blue flight of the kingfisher, scurried into the damp darkness of the river bank with a water vole....

The water-meadows were speckled with molehills. The network of underground passages covered every field, and sometimes if you listened very carefully you could hear the dull scraping of the creatures' spade-like feet as they dug yet another runway. Very rarely, the earth beside you heaved, and a pink-tipped snout broke through, only to retreat hastily underground at the alarming smell of a human.

Unfortunately home-cured mole skins fetched a good price and many of the locals hunted the creatures. The pelts were small and quite a lot were needed to make a shoulder cape or a full-length coat.

10

The year of the storms. How we lost our roof and moved to the village. Why I ran away from home. A night on the moor. A can of pineapple chunks and a litter of kittens. The end of my freedom.

In 1931 I was ten years old. My parents hoped that I would pass the scholarship examination and win a place in a nearby high school for girls but, wisely, they did not press me to work. I was still anaemic and guaranteed to catch any infectious illness that was going round. In January I had chicken-pox, and while I was still in bed the farm-house belonging to the Baker family, at the entrance to Kittiwells, was burned down. Jean and Barbara Baker also had chicken-pox so they were put in bed with me. We passed our time peering from the window excitedly watching the distant smoke of the farm-house, and picking the itchy scabs from each other's spots. All of us were wrapped in red flannel. Country folk firmly believed that this prevented scarring. Certainly, I have no scars nor had the Baker girls.

The weather was shocking throughout most of that year. February and March were cold and wet, and the snow lay thick on Cawsand until late April. The ground was too hard to plant the spring crops. Gusts of icy wind came down from Dartmoor and hurled themselves at the cottage. George Harris's wood-stack collapsed under the onslaught and fell on to Mrs. Worden's hen-house, demolishing it completely.

Two out of a litter of four kittens, born in our linhay one night in April, were frozen to death despite the fact that their mother tried to protect them with her body.

In May, when the thaw came, the drainage ditch behind the cottage was unable to cope with the influx of water from the field and overflowed into our kitchen once more.

Then suddenly it was spring. The air grew warm and balmy. Bluebells crowded the hedgerows, and swallows and house martins built nests under the eaves of our roof. The garden steamed in the sunshine and everything grew wildly, making up for lost time. Along the river bank the lacy flowers of the earth-nut came out in profusion, and each afternoon after school we crowded into the meadow to dig up the tasty white roots. These we wiped more or less clean on our dresses and handkerchiefs, polished them with spittle, and consumed them by the dozen. The weather grew so warm that the tar on the roads softened to an almost liquid state. We walked in it barefoot, enjoying the sensation of the soft heat between our toes, and went home with tar an inch thick coating the soles of our feet. This was removed by the application of paraffin, and during the operation we were thoroughly scolded by our mothers.

But the warm weather did not last. The nights became sharp with frost again, and snow fell at the end of June. The hedgehogs and their young moved indoors and slept in the kitchen.

July was warmer but heavy with thunderstorms. There were reports of floods all along the south coast, and sudden gales blew up. The young apples were stripped from our trees, strawberries and raspberries were blighted, hard, green damsons fell from their branches to litter the ground beneath. Mrs. Worden said delightedly that for the first time in her life there were no "muscrawls" (caterpillars) on the sprout plants.

On the way home from school I hung over Bow Bridge to watch the swirling brown torrent which flowed underneath. It seemed more like winter than summer.

August was cold and wet. A thunderbolt fell harmlessly in Bow village, and onlookers said that it rolled down a gutter—a white-hot ball of fire. Two horses standing together under a tree were struck by lightning. I saw the blackened hooves protruding from under a tarpaulin on the cart that hauled the bodies away.

The month grew colder, and the whole of southern England was swept by winds of hurricane force.

Then, just as all hope of summer had been abandoned, September came in warm and dry. It was far too late to save the hay harvest which had rooted in the fields, but some of the corn which had not been battered to the ground by wind and rain was harvested. A few blackberries ripened in the hedges, and we made blackberry jam. In the morning, sheets of shining gossamer covered the bushes, and in the evenings fat, brown spiders ran into the house seeking winter quarters. The equinox passed quietly but Mrs. Worden sniffed the wind and looked knowledgeably at the distant hills, saying that there was more bad weather ahead. We stocked our shelves with flour and sugar, dried cod and corned beef in case floods made shopping in the village impossible. There was a feeling of tension and expectancy.

The Virginia creeper growing around our front door turned from green to gold, and gold to red; its leaves fell. A last rose blossomed on the ramblers on the garden fence.

In October the weather struck with savage fury. After a day of blue skies and gentle warmth a gale came down from the hills which ripped the thatch from our roof during the night and felled all five of the elm trees across the road. Our upstairs ceilings were soaked with rain-water so that the plaster fell with great thumps.

My parents surveyed the damage with despair. The Harrises, too, had lost most of their thatch and their chimney had come down. Farmer Joslin sent men to cover the cottages with tarpaulins, for the cob walls, exposed to the weather, would have quickly turned to mud and melted away. The drainage ditch again overflowed and flooded our kitchen.

It was too much. I was taken into the village to stay with my grandparents while my mother packed our possessions. A cottage in the main street of the village was empty. It had a septic tank and an outdoor lavatory with a porcelain bowl that could be flushed with a bucket of water. Piped water could be fetched from a stand-pipe across the road. There were two bedrooms, a kitchen/living-room, parlour and a scullery. The roof was slated. It seemed like luxury to us and we could not believe our luck when the landlord rented it to us for five shillings and sixpence per week. There was only one fly in the ointment: most of my pets had to be left behind. The Harrises adopted Skip the sheepdog; the cats, all except one huge black tom called Punch, were dispersed to various farms, and the outdoor animals, hedgehogs and suchlike, were left to fend for themselves.

Punch was transferred to the new house in a large shopping-basket. His paws were buttered and he was shut in the kitchen. He immediately set about licking himself clean; this task took most of a day. The following morning he was allowed out to explore the back garden. Neither he nor I were sure that we liked our new home. After Silver Street it was a "town" house. No longer could we step out of the door almost straight into the fields. Broadnymet Moor was almost three miles away and Dartmoor was dim on the skyline. Much more of my time was spent indoors, and soon I was in trouble.

My mother had bought curtains for our new house because the windows were so much longer than those of the cottage. The new curtains were of Madras lace. On close examination they had a net base on which a design of leaves and flowers was worked by threads loosely pulled through the fabric. I soon found that by pulling an end I could unravel a large patch of the design. The more I ripped the more fascinating it became. One afternoon, when my father was resting and my mother was out, I managed to remove the pattern from the whole of the lower half of a curtain. When my mother came home she completely lost her temper with me. Tired and overwrought with all our troubles, and worried by the expense of settling into the new house, she beat me severely with the back of a hairbrush. Afterwards, I think she was sorry for what she had done but she did not relent with me. I was sent to bed without food and forbidden to tell my father what had happened or to leave the bedroom until she called me. She could not lock me in because there was no key. She had tears in her eyes when she left me.

I realized that I had been naughty but felt that I had been over-punished, and soon my tears gave way to a dull anger. Punch came across the tiles and miaowed at my window. I let him in although I was not allowed to have him in my bedroom: another small crime did not seem to matter. Dimly, in the moonlight I could see Cawsand Beacon silhouetted against the night sky. My heart ached for the peace and quietness of the moor.

Towards midnight I crept downstairs and packed half a loaf of bread, a wedge of cheese and some biscuits in a tea towel. Pinning the bundle to the waist of my dress with a safety-pin, I tucked Punch under my arm and set off.

We went down the long village street and across Bow Bridge. Punch wriggled irritably and then struggled to get free. I had to let him go. He followed me a little way and then vanished into the darkness. I trotted down the North Tawton road, pausing only a minute to look at Silver Street. I would have loved to stay there but I knew it was the first place my parents would look for me.

Soon I left the road and, keeping the rounded hump of Cawsand as my target, scrambled through hedges and across fields. It was rough-going in the fitful moonlight. There were brambles and nettles, ditches, barbed wire, marshy patches and streamlets to cross, but I eventually came to the foot-hills of the moor. Bread and cheese washed down with clear, stream water made a fine breakfast but I was tired, too tired to walk any farther. I slept all day in a grassy clearing surrounded by gorse bushes.

Wortleberries and blackberries with biscuits made an acceptable tea. I set off again climbing upwards. There was a hole in the sole of each of my sandals and the grass, already damp with dew, felt cold to my feet. A buzzard mewed overhead.

Cawsand was looming ahead. I found a stream which ran narrowly and noisily over its gravelly bed and followed it upwards. The moor was menacing with the shades of night. Ponies and sheep sprang from the ground at my approach and darted off into the darkness. I listened to the beat of their hooves and thought of the dreaded Yeth hounds. I hoped that if I heard their distant baying I should be able to find a granite cross to cling to until they had passed. At dawn I settled down to sleep in the ruins of a hut circle on the north-east slopes of Cawsand. The stones were already night-cold and I slept uneasily.

The sun woke me at mid-day and I ate the last of my provisions. Around me the moorland stretched bleak and desolate. The pale, autumn sky yawned to meet the faded heather on the far horizon. The loneliness and the silence were intense. I was afraid, and looked longingly to where the cottages of South Zeal clustered under the hill, but there was no turning back.

Luckily the weather continued fair as I wandered southwards towards Cranmere Pool. That afternoon I sought the company of the ponies grazing in groups between the rock piles. I delighted in the song of a blackbird. Anything which broke the insistent, oppressive silence came as a relief.

That evening I walked until the darkness fell, and then, hungry and cold, came upon a cottage. The woman who answered the door spoke the soft moorland dialect which I could hardly understand. I explained that I was lost and she took me into the kitchen—the only downstairs room—where she fed me with home-baked bread and hot milk. When she heard my story she chided me, and called me a "mazed vule", then set me to sleep, wrapped in blankets on a wooden settle by the fire-place. I did not hear the man of the house come home.

The next morning the husband, Mr. Crocker, said he would take me to a farm where they had a pony and trap. I breakfasted on fried potato cake and a pint of milky cocoa.

It had rained heavily in the night and my feet were very wet by the time we had walked a mile or two across the heather. Already the streamlets were swollen and the ponies stood sullenly along the banks, their manes streaked with rain. It was a fierce but sullen day. The western sky was heavy with cloud and the wind bore a faint taste of salt from the far Atlantic.

The farmer and his wife both scolded me thoroughly but the woman gave me a sticky sandwich of home-made jam and cream, and a large mug of buttermilk to drink.

We went back to Bow along endless unfenced tracks and rutted Devon lanes. I was subdued and anxious about my welcome and very, very cold. It was good to be going home again, in spite of everything.

My parents received me with open arms and insisted that the farmer take a pound note to compensate him for his trouble. Heaven knows what economies had to be practised as a result of that. Punch was already home, having made his way there on the morning after I had left.

I was very quiet for the next few days. The Madras lace curtains still hung at the windows, but I noticed that all the threads making the design had now been pulled out so that the fabric looked like plain net.

The following weekend I developed a chesty cold. It grew rapidly worse and soon I was running a high temperature. Doctor Rowse-Bastard diagnosed bronchitis, which later turned to broncho-pneumonia. I lay inert and apathetic, worn out with coughing, turning my head away from home-made lemonade and beef-tea.

"If she asks for anything let her have it," said the doctor. "Anything to rouse her and make her fight back."

I heard and, as soon as he had gone, asked to see Punch, who was not normally allowed upstairs. He came, and my mother brought with him five little black kittens which belonged to my aunt's cat. They slept on my bed all day, and in the evening I asked for pineapple chunks for my tea. These were fetched from my grandmother's shop. I ate all that were in the can. Within a week I was up and sitting in the window seat. A month later I went back to school.

I still longed for the freedom of Silver Street. It was irksome to have to wear proper clothes instead of running wild in an old cotton dress and sandals. I missed the wild creatures and the sweetness of the fields at dawn and dusk. The village smelled dusty and stale.

The following year we left Bow and moved to the market town of Crediton where I went to school. The standards of conduct required by my new school were very high. The days of my freedom were ended.